KNOWING RIGHT FROM WRONG

KNOWING RIGHT FROM WRONG

KIERAN SETIYA

OXFORD
UNIVERSITY PRESS

OXFORD

UNIVERSITY PRESS

Great Clarendon Street, Oxford, OX2 6DP,
United Kingdom

Oxford University Press is a department of the University of Oxford.
It furthers the University's objective of excellence in research, scholarship,
and education by publishing worldwide. Oxford is a registered trade mark of
Oxford University Press in the UK and in certain other countries

© Kieran Setiya 2012

The moral rights of the author have been asserted

First Edition published in 2012

Impression: 2

British Library Cataloguing in Publication Data

Data available

Library of Congress Cataloging in Publication Data

Data available

ISBN 978-0-19-965745-2

Printed in Great Britain by
CPI Group (UK) Ltd, Croydon, CR0 4YY

Links to third party websites are provided by Oxford in good faith and
for information only. Oxford disclaims any responsibility for the materials
contained in any third party website referenced in this work.

CONTENTS

PREFACE

Though it is not a sequel, this book takes up questions that were not addressed in *Reasons without Rationalism*, and that its argument makes urgent. In that book, I answered a certain sort of ethical sceptic, one who grants that justice and benevolence are virtues, but who asks why he should care. Why bother to act as a virtuous person would? The answer I gave is that the 'should' of reasons cannot be detached from ethical virtue. Its standards are those of good character, applied to practical thought. It follows that, if justice and benevolence are virtues of character, they are responsive to considerations that therefore count as reasons to act. One form of the question 'Why be moral?' is misconceived.

This argument is controversial. Even if it works, however, its limitations are clear. It does not answer a sceptic who grants the authority of virtue but still asks 'Why be moral?' Why believe that justice and benevolence are virtues at all? If they are not, we can act as a virtuous person would while disregarding so-called 'moral virtue' as a sham. Worse yet, there are sceptics who argue that, whatever the truth about virtue and practical reason, our beliefs about them are never justified. In light of disagreement, or problems of reliability and luck, our claims to ethical knowledge are flawed.

It is sceptics of these other kinds that I address in this book. Its arguments are self-contained: they do not rest on my previous work. But there are common themes. One is a denial of normative independence: the standards of reason are not distinct from those of virtue; nor are the standards of epistemology independent of ethical fact. In each case, this prevents a sceptical question from being asked. Along with this parallel, there is the pervasive influence of Aristotle and Hume, and the provocation of Bernard Williams, first through 'Internal and External Reasons', then through *Ethics and the Limits of Philosophy*.

For reactions to this material in earlier forms, I am grateful to audiences at Brown University, the University of Chicago, Columbia University, the University of Illinois, Urbana-Champaign, Johns Hopkins University, the University of Miami, the University of Missouri, St. Louis, the University of Nebraska, the New York Institute of Philosophy, Oxford University, the University of Pittsburgh, Princeton University, Rutgers University, the University of Tennessee, the University of Texas, and the University of Wisconsin, Milwaukee; to participants in graduate seminars on ethical realism and on moral theory at the University of Pittsburgh; and to Ori Beck, Paul Benacerraf, John Broome, David Christensen, Brad Cokelet, Jonathan Dancy, Cian Dorr, Casey Doyle, Antony Eagle, Adam Elga, Matt Evans, Kit Fine, Marah Gubar, Anil Gupta, Mark Hopwood, Paul Horwich, Anja Jauernig, Tom Kelly, Ben Laurence, Brian Leiter, Peter Lewis, John MacFarlane, Colin Marshall, Adam Marushak, John McDowell, Joe Milburn, Dan Morgan, John Morrison, Jessica Moss, Mike Otsuka, Hille Paakkunainen, Joseph Raz, Mark Richard, Gideon Rosen, Karl Schafer, Joshua Schechter, Stephen Schiffer, Nishi Shah, James Shaw, Michael Slote, David Sosa, Nick Stang, Robert Steel, Greg Strom, Scott Sturgeon, Larry Temkin, Katja Vogt, Brian Weatherson, Ralph Wedgwood, Tim Willenken, Mark Wilson, and three anonymous readers for Oxford University Press. Throughout this process, Peter Momtchiloff has been a marvel of efficiency and editorial wisdom. Thanks to the University of Arkansas Press for permission to reproduce, in chapter one, material from my essay, 'Does Moral Theory Corrupt Youth?' (*Philosophical Topics* 38: 1 [Spring 2010]).

It is not uncommon for authors to confess, in the preface to their books, that their writing was a cause of hardship to their family, to apologize for this, and to express their gratitude. The years in which this book were written were not easy ones, but their adversity did not come from the fact that I was writing it. For me, something like the opposite: being absorbed in philosophy, in this work, was a source of solace in difficult times. But not the most important source. In words attributed to Rilke, 'people have misunderstood the position love has in life; they have made it into play and pleasure precisely because they thought that play and pleasure are more blissful than work; but there is nothing happier than work, and love, precisely because it is the supreme happiness, can be nothing other than work'. Marah, this book is for you.

Kieran Setiya

Introduction

One way to prompt doubts about objectivity in ethics is to ask a rhetorical question: if the facts about right and wrong, or what there is reason to do, are independent of my beliefs, how could the truth of those beliefs be anything but luck? Had I been brought up in other ways, at other times, in other places, I would have believed, no less emphatically, quite different things: that it is morally permissible to keep slaves or treat women as property; that justice is a shameful vice; that there is reason to do only what is in one's own best interests, regardless of its effects on others, or to maximize utility, even though some are trampled along the way. Though my beliefs would have been different, the facts would not have changed. They do not depend on me. Instead, my beliefs would have been false. Is it simply my good fortune to believe the truth?

The anxiety elicited here can take quite different forms. Why is it disturbing to suppose that our access to ethical truth depends on luck? One answer cites the epistemic significance of disagreement. I do not hold the terrible views described above, but what could I say to someone who does? Our disagreements are sufficiently deep that any argument I could give would beg the question. I have no independent grounds on which to discount his views, or to treat myself as more reliable. How can I then persist in my convictions? How can I think that I am the one who happens to be right?

We can press the point in other ways. If I am reliable in ethics, there is a systematic correlation of fact and belief: of what is right and wrong, or what there is reason to do, on one side, and my psychology, on the other. If the facts are independent of what I think, how could this correlation be explained? It is a mere coincidence, miraculous, convenient, and, on reflection, quite impossible to believe.[1]

Nor do I simply aspire to justification. Much of what I hold in ethics I take to be not merely true, and justified, but known. I do not merely think that slavery is wrong, I know it is. I know that women are not the property of men, that there is reason to care about people other than myself, that one should respect the rights of the innocent even at some cost to the greater good. If I know these things, the truth of my beliefs is not an accident; it can somehow be explained. Yet if the facts are independent of me, what could this explanation be?

This book confronts the threat to objectivity in ethics posed by epistemic luck, teasing out its separate threads. There is the problem of ethical disagreement, which is the topic of chapter one. There is the problem of reliability and coincidence, which is the topic of chapter two. And there is the problem of knowledge and accidental truth, which is the topic of chapter three. In solving these problems, I argue against epistemologies of intuition, coherence, and reflective equilibrium; I argue that the basic standards of epistemology in ethics are biased towards the truth; I argue that there is ethical knowledge only if our beliefs are constitutively bound up with the facts; and I argue that we can accept all this, without implausible predictions of convergence or relativity, through a synthesis of Aristotle and Hume.

---

[1] This style of argument is inspired by Hartry Field (Field 1989: 25–30, 230–9).

1. PLAN OF THIS BOOK

Before giving a more detailed outline of my argument, I introduce some claims I won't attempt to argue for. Although my premises are modest, they are not indisputable: they represent the framework of the book and a limitation of its scope. This is not a comprehensive treatise in the metaphysics and epistemology of ethics, though it has a lot to say about both. It is a response to the most challenging and intractable forms of ethical scepticism.

What do I mean by 'ethics'? I want to be inclusive. There are claims of right and wrong, and of what there is reason to do, but there are practical reasons of other kinds—reasons for wanting, respecting, or admiring things—along with claims of virtue and vice, acting well or badly, moral obligation, justice, benevolence, courage, and the rest. A rule of thumb, to which I return below: if in doubt, it's ethical.

I assume at the outset that we can speak of ethical claims or propositions, as I have done; that they can be true or false; and that we aspire to knowledge in our ethical beliefs. Though they suggest a form of 'cognitivism', these assumptions may be shared by contemporary 'expressivists' and 'quasi-realists'.[2] They do not presuppose a particular interpretation of truth or belief.

Since we can be wrong in our beliefs, there is scope for ethical disagreement. I assume that this is possible even among those who belong to quite different communities. It is not that we cannot talk past each other, but mostly we do not. Exceptions aside, when we seem to disagree in ethics, we do: at least one of us must be mistaken—though not, perhaps, irrational—in his beliefs. This premise rules out one form of relativism. But it is ecumenical. Some so-called 'relativists' aim to accommodate

---

[2] See Blackburn 1993, 1998; Gibbard 1990, 2003. For the same reason, I doubt that the issues raised in Fine 2001 are directly relevant here.

disagreement between different communities and their members; they can accept what I assume.[3]

A final premise is familiar, but more complex: it is a version of ethical supervenience. The core idea of supervenience is that ethical differences turn on differences of other kinds, that ethical concepts apply in virtue of others. If I acted wrongly and you did not, there must be something to say about why: about the action I performed, its causes or effects, the intention with which it was performed, its content or context, that explains the ethical contrast, facts in virtue of which my action was wrong and yours was not. If there is a reason for me to act which is not a reason for you, there must be a difference between my circumstance and yours from which this ethical difference flows. Likewise for virtue and vice. If you are temperate and I am not, there must be psychological differences between us that underlie this fact. The proper formulation of supervenience involves substantive difficulties, which are taken up below in section 2. What we need for now is the core idea.

With these assumptions, we turn back to our principal theme. This book works through a series of sceptical arguments that appeal to epistemic luck, as it appears in disagreement, in the claim to reliability, and in accidental truth. These arguments question our entitlement to believe, or claim to know, the ethical facts. They do not aim to refute, directly, the existence of such facts.[4] In answering them, I will ask what must be true about the structure of justification and the nature of ethics if we have ethical knowledge or justified belief. Although I defend these conditions, and believe they can be met, I will not argue for them on independent grounds. The case for my conclusions is

[3] I am thinking here of recent work by John MacFarlane (2005, 2007) and Mark Richard (2008: Chs. 4–5).

[4] In this respect, they differ from the metaphysical version of Mackie's 'argument from queerness', on which there is something problematic in the very idea of an objectively prescriptive fact; see Mackie 1977: 38–42.

that we must accept them if we are to avoid the prospect of ethical scepticism.

Thus, in chapter one, I assume that we should persist in true beliefs even in the face of intractable disagreement. Confronted with those who deny that justice and benevolence are virtues, that there is reason to care about anyone but oneself, the proper response is to hold one's ground. Having clarified this view, I explore its implications for evidence in ethics. One consequence is that the evidence for ethical beliefs does not consist in ethical intuitions; nor is justification a matter of reflective equilibrium or coherence among beliefs. In order to resist the inference from fundamental disagreement to scepticism, we must reject these influential pictures of justification in ethical theory. What we need instead is a conception of justified belief on which the evidence for ethical claims is fundamentally non-ethical: it is evidence for facts on which the truth in ethics supervenes. This view contrasts with a second form of intuitionism, which draws not on intuitions as evidence, but on self-evident principles or non-evidentially justified beliefs. In defending the evidential view, I engage with traditional debates in epistemology, about coherence and foundationalism, and about the relationship of justification to truth.

Despite its scope, chapter one leaves many unanswered questions. To know the evidence for ethical beliefs is not to know when such beliefs are justified, if ever. There is more to justification than evidence. Chapter two advances the discussion in three ways. First, it addresses the objection that forming ethical beliefs on non-ethical grounds is in violation of a Humean constraint: no inferring 'ought' from 'is'.[5] I argue that the deductive model of justification behind this complaint is generally flawed, and I explore the role of reliability in forming justified beliefs.

---

[5] Hume, *Treatise* 3.1.1.27. Whether Hume accepts the constraint is a matter of dispute.

The second task of chapter two is to refute an argument against 'ethical realism'—roughly, the independence of ethical fact and belief—according to which it makes our reliability in ethics a sheer coincidence.[6] The correlation of ethical fact and belief is held by the critic to be incredible unless it can be explained, which ethical realism precludes. In response, I argue that we are justified in accepting a coincidence, without the need for explanation, if we have sufficient evidence of its occurrence. According to the theory of chapter one, that is our situation in the ethical case. Finally, I show that there is nothing circular in this account. It does not beg the question to argue for reliability in ethics by way of ethical beliefs.

The sceptical problems considered in the first two chapters turn on misconceptions in epistemology. They can be solved in epistemic terms: by determining what counts as evidence in ethics, and what is involved in begging the question. These solutions have no metaphysical upshot. They are consistent with the irreducibility of ethical facts, their causal impotence, and their constitutive independence of us. In chapter three, we confront a less tractable argument, about the conditions of knowledge as non-accidentally true belief. When S knows that p, I argue, she knows it by a reliable method, and her reliability is no accident. There is a connection between her using method m and its being reliable. The challenge in ethics is to meet this condition. What does the reliability of our methods have to do with the fact that we use them?

This demand has metaphysical implications. Unless our beliefs are constitutively bound to ethical facts—or aligned with them by an accommodating God—our use of reliable methods in ethics cannot be explained. So, at least, I attempt to show. This conclusion leaves room for constitutive theories of opposing kinds, some 'constructivist', explaining the facts in terms of our beliefs, others 'externalist', explaining our beliefs partly in terms of a tendency

---

[6] Here I am concerned especially with the work of Sharon Street (2006, ms.).

to match the facts. The fundamental question for such accounts is how to connect fact with belief, in either direction, without falling into relativism or predicting an implausible measure of convergence in ethical thought. Here disagreement returns as a constraint on theory. If there is a common subject matter about which individuals and communities disagree, sometimes in radical ways, the facts involved cannot be too closely bound to what any of them believe. At the same time, the connection of fact and attitude must be strong enough to explain the reliability of some.

In chapter four, I try to reconcile these conflicting claims. If ethical facts are bound to our beliefs through the natural history of human life, I argue, it is no accident that we are ethically reliable, when we are. At the same time, there is room for individuals and even whole societies to go astray. If ethical knowledge is possible, despite the limits of convergence, it is explained by human nature. The argument of the book thus leads, in a new way, to a traditional view: that ethical knowledge needs foundations, and that unless they are merely social, they must be found in human nature, in the nature of reason, or in God. My approach is secular, and I argue against foundations in reason. If we hope to save ethical objectivity, human nature is the only place to turn.

The closing sections of the book explore the metaphysics of human nature, along with its empirical study. Does the doctrine of what I call 'natural reliability' conflict with what is empirically known about the diversity of ethical belief? I argue that it does not, though my argument rests in part on the poverty of existing work. Our empirical knowledge of human nature is thin. I also confront a final issue, about knowledge and justification. Unlike the arguments of chapters one and two, the argument from non-accidental truth bears specifically on what we know. Is there room to give up on ethical knowledge while saving justified belief? Not on the assumption, which I defend, that justified belief turns on the capacity to know. If ethical knowledge is impossible, we are not entitled to ethical belief. The task of this book is to expose and defend the conditions under which, against the threat of epistemic luck, we can lay claim to both.

2. ETHICAL SUPERVENIENCE

The supervenience of the ethical lies in the background of our discussion, especially in chapter one. According to the doctrine of supervenience, ethical differences turn on differences of other kinds; ethical concepts apply in virtue of others. But what exactly does this mean? The idea of ethical supervenience can be developed in several ways, some of which raise serious problems. The purpose of this section is to work these problems out.[7]

It might be thought, to begin with, that the ethical supervenes on the 'natural': no difference in the ethical properties of an act or agent without a corresponding difference in their natural properties. The trouble is to find an account of the natural, a way of classifying properties as natural or not, on which it is safe to assume that ethical properties are not themselves natural. If natural properties are those with causal powers, it is controversial to suppose that ethical properties are not: that they are causally inert. If natural properties are the subject matter of the natural and social sciences, reductive naturalists will hold that they include the ethical.[8] If being right is maximizing pleasure, the property of being right is ethical and natural at once. The idea that ethical properties are natural properties is not an objection to super-venience. The problem is rather that it makes the supervenience of the ethical on the natural entirely trivial. It fails to capture the

---

[7] In writing it, I have been helped by Sturgeon 2009, which provides more detailed references and deals with some distinctions I neglect.

[8] What do I mean by 'reductive naturalism'? Since I do not use the term in the principal chapters, and since I drop the idea of a natural property as unhelpful, I leave the details for others. A rough conception will suffice.

intended thought: that ethical differences depend on differences of other kinds.

A more promising line is that the ethical supervenes on the non-ethical, but this too will need revision. The difficulty stems, again, from reductive naturalism. If being right is maximizing pleasure, the property of maximizing pleasure should count as an ethical property. It is picked out by an ethical concept, the concept of being right. It follows, if ethical properties supervene on others, that there can be no difference in what maximizes pleasure without a difference of some other kind. There is, however, no reason to assume, as an implication of ethical supervenience and reductive naturalism, that maximizing pleasure supervenes on anything else. If the doctrine of supervenience is to accommodate this, it must be formulated in some other way.[9]

The solution, I think, is to shift from properties to concepts, constituents of propositions.[10] Even if being F is being G, the proposition that x is F may be distinct from the proposition that x is G, and the corresponding concepts not the same. We begin, then, with ethical concepts: *right, wrong, practical reason, acting well or badly, moral obligation, justice, benevolence, courage*. As before, the safest rule of classification is: if in doubt, it's ethical. A case of particular importance, and a partial exception to this: concepts of non-factive attitudes, like belief, with ethical content, are not ethical. In the relevant sense, that someone believes that slavery is wrong is not an ethical proposition, unlike the fact that he knows this to be true. Ethical beliefs are among the facts on which the ethical supervenes: they are relevant to virtue and vice.

Ethical concepts in hand, we can formulate a principle of possible variation:

---

[9] This point is made, at greater length, by Nicholas Sturgeon (2009: 69–73).

[10] Where propositions are Fregean thoughts, individuated by sense or mode of presentation. Russellian theorists must adapt this solution to their view.

There can be no difference in the ethical concepts that apply to acts or agents without a difference in the non-ethical concepts that apply to them.

But there is a risk of triviality, again. If the concept, *thinking it is wrong*, is not an ethical concept, and the concept *truth* is not, what about the concept, *being such that if someone had believed that it was wrong, their belief would have been true*? If this too is non-ethical, we can manufacture non-ethical concepts to ensure the truth of supervenience without respecting its intended force. There are various ways in which one might respond to this, for instance, by insisting that a concept can be ethical even when its component concepts are not. A simpler point is that the idea of ethical supervenience is an idea of dependence, not mere correlation, and the application of the counterfactual concept above is never what makes an action wrong. What is true, without being trivial, is this:

ETHICAL SUPERVENIENCE: If an act or agent falls under ethical concept, E, it does so in virtue of falling under non-ethical concepts, N, such that necessarily, what falls under N falls under E.

This principle does preclude a certain form of naturalism. It is consistent with Ethical Supervenience that the nature of ethical properties can be fully expressed with non-ethical concepts, as in the doctrine that being right is maximizing pleasure. More generally, there is room for:

REDUCTIONISM: For every ethical concept, E, there are non-ethical concepts, N, with which we can say what it is to have the property picked out by E.

What is not consistent with Supervenience, or what would make it problematic, is that the concept, *being right*, just is the concept, *maximizing pleasure*. That would make the concept, *maximizing pleasure*, ethical, and Ethical Supervenience would claim that its application supervenes on something else. That is not required for the supervenience of the ethical. If we want to allow for reductive naturalism at the level of concepts, not just properties, we must revise our principle again.

My response is to deny the antecedent. We began with a generous list of ethical concepts: *right, wrong, practical reason, acting well or badly, moral obligation, justice, benevolence, courage,* and more. That these concepts are identical to ones that fall outside the list is quite implausible. The proposition that x is right is not the proposition that it maximizes pleasure: these are different objects of belief. Moore's open question argument, according to which it is intelligible to ask, for any such equation, 'It is N, but is it E?' may not do much to prove this.[11] (Is intelligibility a sure test of concept identity? How can we generalize from the intelligibility of the questions we have considered so far to the intelligibility of all?) But the relevant conclusion holds: ethical concepts form a limited class, divined by our inclusive list; and what is not on the list is not an ethical concept. It is to ethical concepts, so conceived, that Supervenience applies.

[11] Moore 1903: Ch. 1.

1

Disagreement

How far should my ethical beliefs be shaken or undermined by the discovery that others, no less intelligent than I am, no less thoughtful, no less informed in other respects, disagree with me in radical ways? According to a tempting account of the epistemology of disagreement in general, the answer is that my confidence should fade. In *The Methods of Ethics*, Sidgwick wrote:

[If] I find any of my judgements, intuitive or inferential, in direct conflict with a judgement of some other mind, there must be error somewhere: and if I have no more reason to suspect error in the other mind than in my own, reflective comparison between the two judgements necessarily reduces me temporarily to a state of neutrality. And although the total result in my mind is not exactly suspense of judgement, but an alternation and conflict between positive affirmation by one act of thought and the neutrality that is the result of another, it is obviously something very different from scientific certitude. (Sidgwick 1907: 342)

Sidgwick's position is evidently nuanced, but it is in the vicinity of a simpler view, that the correct response to disagreement with an 'epistemic peer' is to become agnostic about the matters on which we disagree. The danger is that, in ethics, disagreement with peers is more or less routine; it is then the basis of a devastating scepticism.

Before dissecting this argument, we should pause to examine its premise. In light of Ethical Supervenience, we know that, if an act or agent falls under an ethical concept, it does so in virtue of falling under non-ethical concepts, the application of which entails that the ethical concept applies. Entailment here is metaphysical necessity: necessarily, if x is N then x is E. For the sake of this discussion, a case of fundamental disagreement is one in which I believe that x is E, you believe that it is not, but we agree that x is N; or one in which I believe that if x is N then x is E, but you deny it. In effect, we disagree about the ethical import of non-ethical facts that entail an ethical proposition. Is fundamental disagreement possible? And does it actually occur?

To take the question of possibility first: some accounts of moral concept-possession imply that there are limits, perhaps quite stringent ones, on the extent to which we can disagree. According to Frank Jackson, the content of our concepts depends on what we take for granted about their application, the platitudes that govern their use. Thus, 'moral disagreement', while possible, 'requires a background of shared moral opinion to fix a common . . . set of meanings for our moral terms' (Jackson 1998: 132). If we appear to disagree too sharply, the right interpretation is that we are talking past each other, expressing different concepts even if we use the same words.[1] The scope for genuine disagreement is narrow.

There is some plausibility in this. As Philippa Foot observed, if someone proclaims as an 'ultimate principle [that it is] wrong to run around trees right handed or to look at hedgehogs in the light of the moon', we will doubt that he grasps the concepts of moral right and wrong (Foot 2002: xiv).[2] In the case of morality, or with concepts of particular virtues, substantial agreement may be required. If you do not know that benevolence has to do with helping people, or courage with fear, do you have these concepts at all?

What I deny is that concept-possession is so constrained as to prevent us from disagreeing about ethics in ways that are both

---

[1] Jackson 1998: 137.

[2] Foot makes earlier versions of this point in her 1958: 107; 1958–9: 119. For resistance, see Miller 1985: 523–6.

pervasive and fundamental.[3] This case could be made in general, or with any given concept, but it is especially clear with the concept of a reason for action or what there is reason to do, and the correlative sense of 'should'. The range of views that have been taken here is extraordinarily wide. Some hold an egoistic theory of practical reason, on which one should act so as to maximize net benefit to oneself. The only reason to do something is that it will be good for you.[4] Others object that we should be impartial between what benefits us and what benefits anyone else: one should act so as to maximize net benefit to all.[5] Some object in the opposite way: 'I do not see why the axiom of Prudence should not be questioned, when it conflicts with present inclination, on a ground similar to that on which Egoists refuse to admit the axiom of Rational Benevolence' (Sidgwick 1907: 418).[6] On an influential form of instrumentalism about practical reason, reasons for action derive always and exclusively from our final desires.[7] If I do not care about my future interests or my present needs, I have no reason to bother with them. Yet this, too, has been denied. While for Bernard Williams, '[desiring] to do something is of course a reason for doing it' (Williams 1985: 19), for Derek Parfit, 'the fact that we have some desire never, by itself, provides reasons' (Parfit 1997: 128).[8] The upshot of this wild and perhaps disturbing fragmentation is that, whatever the truth about reasons for action, there is someone to deny it. Even if they knew the relevant non-ethical facts, the proponents of these views would disagree about a vast array of cases. At least one of them would thus dispute

[3] Again, see Miller 1985: 531–48; also Wedgwood 2010: 217–18.

[4] On the history of this idea in moral philosophy, see Shaver 1999.

[5] Nagel 1970 defends impartiality or agent-neutrality as a principle of practical reason.

[6] Though he raised this question, Sidgwick was himself disposed to the rationality of altruism.

[7] Instrumentalist theories are proposed in Gauthier 1986: Ch. II; Dreier 1997; Hubin 1999, 2001; and, with qualifications, in Williams 1979.

[8] For similar claims, see Broome 1997; Scanlon 1998: Ch. 1; Parfit 2011: Chs. 3–4.

the truth. Fundamental disagreement about what there is reason to do, and what one should do, all things considered, is surely possible.

Is it actual? Since there have been advocates of self-interest, altruism, and desire in the theory of practical reason, the only obstacle to disagreements of this kind is ignorance of non-ethical fact. If we are not aware that x is N, where necessarily, if x is N then x is E, we cannot engage in fundamental disagreement as it was previously defined. But this is superficial. As we will see, what matters in ethical disagreement is that, among those who disagree with me, some would continue to disagree even if they were non-ethically informed. And this, again, is surely true.

This chapter examines the prospects for a sceptical argument from disagreement in ethics. What must be true for this argument to work? What are the costs, or implications, of resistance? In section 1, I argue that we can and should reject conciliatory accounts of disagreement in general. If there is a sceptical problem in ethics, it rests on more specific claims about the grounds of ethical belief. In section 2, I turn to epistemologies of intuition, coherence, and reflective equilibrium. Though influential, these views are seriously flawed: confronted with disagreement, they lead to scepticism; or they avoid it in implausible ways. As I argue in section 3, the problem of disagreement can be solved without implausibility only if the basic standards of epistemology in ethics are biased towards the truth. I end by explaining what this means.

1. EQUAL WEIGHT

In 'Reflection and Disagreement', Adam Elga defends a concessive view of disagreement with advisors and peers.

Upon finding out that an advisor disagrees, your probability that you are right should equal your prior conditional probability that you would be right. Prior to what? Prior to thinking through the disputed issue, and finding out what the advisor thinks of it. Conditional on what? On whatever you have learned about the circumstances of disagreement. (Elga 2007: 490)[9]

According to this Equal Weight View, when I believe p and learn that you believe the opposite, I should ask myself: when I set aside the reasoning that persuades me of p, how likely is it that, in the relevant circumstance, my belief would be correct? It is crucial that the circumstance 'should be individuated just coarsely enough so that the relevant conditional probability judgment is genuinely prior to [my] reasoning about the disputed issue' (Elga 2007: 490). In other words, the relevant circumstance cannot include the grounds on which I believe p, though it can include such facts as that the advisor's belief strikes me as insane. This is how Elga accommodates the case in which we split the bill after dinner, I come up with \$28, and you come up with \$280, without concluding that I should change my mind. My conditional credence that I am right, if your answer seems to me not only wrong but mad, is relatively high.[10]

Elga's formulation of the Equal Weight View, while elegant, is incomplete. The quoted principle specifies what some of my credences should become, while leaving others indeterminate. It could be filled out in various ways. These complications will not matter for our discussion. The Equal Weight View represents, for us, the policy of deference to advisors and peers; we need not be too specific about the form such deference takes.

One clarification is, however, crucial. As it stands, the Equal Weight View cites the prior conditional credence I actually have. It ignores the possibility that my credence is unwarranted, as for instance that it contradicts my evidence. But we cannot ignore

---

[9] Similar views are proposed by Richard Feldman (2006) and David Christensen (2007).

[10] Compare Christensen 2007: 199–203.

this. If am irrationally confident of my own reliability, my credence in p conditional on my believing it while you do not may be extremely high, even when I set aside the reasoning that persuades me of p. It does not follow that I *should* be confident that I am right when we turn out to disagree. My degrees of belief are not so easily laundered of epistemic dirt. In order to avoid this implication, we should state the Equal Weight View as follows:

Upon finding out that an advisor disagrees with you about p, your credence in p should become what your prior conditional credence should have been, where 'prior' means prior to thinking through the disputed issue and 'conditional' means conditional on whatever you have learned about the circumstances of disagreement, excluding the grounds on which your confidence in p is based.

One virtue of this formulation is that it is extremely general. It treats Sidgwick's claim about epistemic equals as a special case of deference to advisors one should regard as more or less reliable. It also defines their position in terms of the prior conditional credence one should have, not by reference to degree of 'familiarity with the evidence and arguments that bear on [a] question' and the comparative possession of 'general epistemic virtues such as intelligence, thoughtfulness, and freedom from bias' (Kelly 2005: 174–5). The Equal Weight View does not imply that, if we meet these informal conditions to the same degree, I should be no more confident that I will get things right when our opinions diverge. In general, it takes no stand on the qualities one's prior conditional credence should reflect.

At the same time, there is room to argue for sceptical conclusions from the Equal Weight View, given premises of this form:

Some of those who disagree with me about ethical proposition p are *epistemic peers*, in that my prior conditional credence in p—prior to thinking through the disputed issue and conditional on the circumstances of disagreement—should be relatively low.

Such premises can be tempting. In a case of fundamental disagreement, how can I deny that you are an epistemic peer? I cannot discount your view by pointing to your ignorance outside of ethics, since we agree on the relevant facts. Can I appeal to ethical beliefs, disputing your reliability on the ground that you are wrong about ethical matters other than *p*? If we disagree about a whole array of topics in ethics, about rights and consequences, liberty and welfare, my prior conditional credence in some further claim—say, about the permissibility of euthanasia—given that I accept it and you do not, may be relatively high.[11] Even before I think through the disputed issue, I am justly confident that, if we were to disagree, it is your belief that would be false. But there is an obvious response: we should include the further topics of disagreement in the content of the proposition on which we disagree, focusing not on the permissibility of euthanasia, but on our conflicting systems of ethical belief. How can I deny that, in this larger disagreement, you are an epistemic peer? How can I be confident that my belief would be true, prior to thinking through the disputed issue, and apart from the grounds, ethical and otherwise, on which our opposing convictions rest? If we disagree about a proposition, and we are epistemic peers, the Equal Weight View tells me to relinquish my belief. It threatens to push us from disagreement to scepticism.

This argument has two premises: that in a given disagreement, we are epistemic peers; and that the Equal Weight View holds. The depth of its sceptical impact turns on the extent to which we disagree. If disagreement between peers is sufficiently rare, we might accept the conclusion: a qualified ethical scepticism. It is not troubling to concede that certain questions in ethics are so controversial, so difficult to resolve, that we should doubt that we have got them right. To reinforce this complacency, we might add that the Equal Weight response to disagreement turns, in ways

---

[11] See Elga 2007: 492–4.

that have so far not been specified, on the number of peers with whom we disagree. If we are to defer to epistemic peers as guides or indicators of the truth, we should do so in proportion to their frequency, or in proportion to the frequency of independent views.[12] It is only when disagreement is both fundamental and sufficiently widespread that our confidence should be swamped by dissent. The sceptical force of the Equal Weight View is thus contained.

What should we make of this? Is there a sceptical problem or not? To answer these questions directly, we would need to know the extent of actual disagreement in ethics, the extent to which it is fundamental, the extent to which it reflects our independent views, and so on. These are anthropological matters of enormous complexity.[13] But we do not need to engage with them in order to see that something has gone wrong. We can ask instead what our premises imply about metaphysical possibilities. Suppose, for instance, you belong to a homogeneous community whose ethical beliefs are true and who are non-ethically well-informed. For the first time, you meet a stranger. He agrees with you outside of ethics, but when it comes to practical reason, his beliefs are shocking. Fill in the details as you like. Perhaps he thinks we should act on our final desires, whatever they are, that we should be utterly selfish, that we should maximize aggregate happiness, no matter who is trampled on the way. It turns out that he, too, belongs to a homogeneous community, exactly as numerous as your own. What should you now believe? Your disagreement is fundamental. If the stranger is your epistemic peer, and the Equal Weight View holds, you should lose faith in your ethical beliefs: you should become agnostic about the matters on which you

---

[12] The need for independence is emphasized in Kelly 2010: 146–9; see also McGrath 2008: 94–5.

[13] For an introduction to these disputes, see Moody-Adams 1997: Chs. 1–2; Doris and Plakias 2008. We return to the anthropology of disagreement in chapters three and four.

disagree. But that is not the right response! We should not defer to moral monsters but condemn them, however numerous they are. It is no surprise that people can be depraved: they can deny the truth in fundamental ways. Meeting them, and counting them, should not shake your confidence in the facts. We should not act on vicious desires, be thoroughly selfish, ignore the rights of the innocent, and we should be confident of this even if others disagree. In confrontations of this kind, our premises give the wrong result.

The upshot is this: on the Equal Weight View, I can cling to the truth in ethics, faced with fundamental disagreement, only if my prior conditional credence in my ethical outlook should be relatively high.[14] I must be entitled to confidence in my beliefs, even apart from the evidence on which they rest. Some will be happy to assert this: their views are taken up below.[15] What I want to stress now is that one need not share them in order to block the sceptical inference. Whatever we make of prior probabilities in ethics, we can reject the inference by showing that its other premise fails.

In a recent essay on disagreement, Tom Kelly argues convincingly that we should not accept the Equal Weight View.[16] His most compelling objection is this: in saying that I should become

[14] Mere indeterminacy is not enough (compare Elga 2007: 495–6). While the Equal Weight View could be stated so as to give no advice when it is indeterminate what one's prior conditional credence should be, or when it should have no determinate value, or when it should involve a kind of uncertainty that cannot be modelled in probabilistic terms, these restrictions are ad hoc. The idea behind the view is that one's post-confrontation credence should match what one's prior conditional credence should have been. Indeterminacy in the latter should be tracked by indeterminacy in the former. On this basis, the sceptical inference can be revived: not that your credence should be low, in the face of radical disagreement, but that it is indeterminate what it should be, or that it should be indeterminate, or that you should be totally unsure—different kinds of sceptical result, perhaps, but no better than the one we feared.

[15] Variations include the kind of egoism derived and rejected in section 2, and the non-evidential form of intuitionism considered in section 3.

[16] Kelly 2010: §3. He also gives a sound response to Elga's principal argument; see Kelly 2010: §5.4 on Elga 2007: 487. Because I am persuaded by Kelly's discussion, the treatment in the text is brief.

agnostic when I disagree with peers, the Equal Weight View gives too little weight to the prior evidence for my belief. On the Equal Weight View, this evidence is effectively 'screened off' by the fact that we disagree. It as if I have nothing to go on but our present opinions and their prior probabilities of being right: the actual grounds of my belief have disappeared. As Kelly points out, however, this is not the case.

The mistake in the Equal Weight verdict is especially clear when we share the same evidence. Suppose that we are trained in meteorology, and that we are equally competent: my prior conditional credence that it will rain today given that I come to that conclusion and you do not is, and should be, about a half. We each consult the same reports and satellite photographs. On this basis, I am convinced that it will rain. To my surprise, you do not agree. What should I think? If our shared evidence in fact supports the conclusion that it will rain, and you are simply wrong, I should not lose confidence altogether. Perhaps I ought to be a bit less sure, but the balance of evidence remains with me. Your belief is evidence that it will not rain, like the evidence supplied by a reliable barometer. It is no more than that. The fact that you disagree is not sufficient to silence or outweigh the body of data that indicates rain, which my beliefs should continue to track.

It is helpful to compare my situation with that of a third party who has nothing to go on but the fact that we disagree. After learning what happened, the observer should be agnostic about the weather. He has no access to the primary evidence and no way to break the symmetry between us. On the Equal Weight View, my situation is no better: I should be no more confident that it will rain, on the basis of the evidence and the fact of your dissent, than on the basis of our beliefs alone; I cannot give the evidence, however strong, more weight than the bare fact of my belief. There is no reason to think that the weight of evidence is so constrained.

According to the picture I am defending, our situation is enduringly asymmetric. If the evidence supports my view before we meet, you should not have made the opposite prediction; nor should I be strongly moved by your dissent. This verdict may seem unfair. After all, things will seem to you just as they do to me, as though the evidence is on your side and your interlocutor has been misled. But the asymmetry is real. It is a mistake to suppose that the weight of evidence is fixed by how it seems, even to thoughtful and reflective subjects, or that I should ignore the evidence I have.

Nor should I be deterred by the reappearance of disagreement through epistemic ascent. In the weather case, we are likely to have conflicting beliefs not only about the rain, but about the weight of evidence. I think it supports my view; you think it supports yours. This prompts a rejoinder, due to Richard Feldman.[17] I know that one of us is wrong about the weight of evidence. In light of our symmetry, how can I be justified in thinking that it is you? We need not answer this question directly in order to state the basic response. What Feldman needs is an argument from disagreement to scepticism for epistemic beliefs: since we disagree about the weight of evidence, I am not entitled to believe that I am right. The only argument of this kind we have seen is one that assumes the Equal Weight View. We cannot rely on this argument in defending that view.[18] More generally, we cannot endorse the inference from disagreement to doubt in epistemology unless we are willing to endorse it elsewhere. And as I argued above, it is a mistake to do so in the ethical case.

The moral to draw at this point is that there is no hope for a general argument from epistemic peers in ethics to ethical scepticism. An argument of this kind would have to assume the Equal Weight View; and the Equal Weight View fails. It is striking,

---

[17] Feldman 2006: 231–2; see also Christensen 2007: 196–7.

[18] For a more extensive reply, with which I am sympathetic, see Kelly 2010: 155–60.

however, that we have reached this conclusion in a completely abstract way. We have done so on the basis of an objection—that the Equal Weight View underestimates the force of prior evidence—that has nothing to do with ethics in particular. What is more, we have done so without explaining how ethical beliefs are justified, when they are. What evidence do we have for such beliefs? Do they rest on evidence at all? Until we address these questions, the most we can say is that a sceptical argument from disagreement in ethics would have to engage them. Its cogency depends on the structure of justification for ethical belief.

As we will see, the threat implicit in these remarks is credible. There are influential theories of evidence in ethics, and of the shape of ethical inquiry, on which the sceptical problem is renewed, or on which it is prevented in dubious ways. Responding to these conceptions—what do we have to say about the episte-mology of ethics in order to avoid them?—establishes the frame-work for the rest of the book.

2. INTUITIONS, COHERENCE, REFLECTIVE EQUILIBRIUM

According to some philosophers, the fundamental data for ethical theory are intuitions, conceived as cognitive states that are not beliefs—they are appearances, or inclinations to believe—in which ethical propositions are presented to us as true. For Shelly Kagan, 'intuitions about cases provide us with *evidence* for and against rival moral claims—and it is difficult to imagine giving them no weight whatsoever' (Kagan 2001: 45). Although he is initially concerned with intuitions about cases, not about general principles, Kagan thinks we have both. The justification of ethical belief begins, but does not end, with intuitions of these kinds. Its further target is coherence: so far as possible, our ethical outlook should consist of a simple, consistent body of principles that supports and explains our particular verdicts. The theoretical virtues of simplicity, power, and explanatory depth must be weighed against fidelity to intuition.[19] The proper balance of these factors tells us what we should believe.

As Kagan suggests, this picture sees ethical thought as broadly analogous to empirical.[20] It treats our intuitions as a matter of how things seem, ethically speaking, and gives them the epistemic role of perceptual appearances. Thomas Nagel defends this analogy in *The View from Nowhere*:

In physics, one infers from factual appearances to their most plausible explanation in a theory of how the world is. In ethics, one infers from appearances of value to their most plausible explanation in a theory of what there is reason to do or want.... If we start by regarding the appearances of value as appearances of something, and then step back to form hypotheses about the broader system of motivational possibilities of which we have had a glimpse, the result is a gradual opening out of a complex domain which we apparently discover. The method of discovery is to seek the best normative explanation of the normative appearances. (Nagel 1986: 146)

In the background of this Empirical Model is an epistemological theory on which one's degrees of belief should be proportioned to one's evidence; and one's evidence is identified with a set of propositions or attitudes to which one bears some special relation. The indeterminacies of this theory could be resolved in various ways. As it stands, it does not say that one should be confident of *p* only if one has evidence of its truth: there is room for non-evidentially justified beliefs. Nor does it entail 'objective Bayesianism', according to which one's degrees of belief should match permissible prior probabilities conditionalized on evidence propositions. It assumes little or nothing about the nature of evidence

---

[19] For the list of virtues here, see Kagan 1989: 11–14.
[20] Kagan 2001: §II.

and evidential support. What the Empirical Model adds to this abstract theory is that, for ethical beliefs, one's evidence is ultimately supplied by ethical intuitions, and that the 'proportions' that one's degrees of belief should bear to this evidence are fixed by permissible standards of coherence and of deference to how things seem.

Two complications are worth noting. The first is that some ethical beliefs, and perhaps some intuitions, rest on beliefs whose content is not ethical. Suppose I think you should quit your job because it makes you unhappy. If the latter belief is unjustified, that will tend to undermine the former. The crucial point is that, on the Empirical Model, this is the only way in which non-ethical evidence is relevant to ethical beliefs. Your ethical beliefs are justified if they rest on justified non-ethical beliefs and they are proportioned to your ethical intuitions. The second complication comes from testimony, which may provide a source of evidence absent from the model above. Since I will be arguing that there is a problem of disagreement for the Empirical Model, and since giving direct weight to testimony would only make this problem worse, it is harmless to ignore it here.

Although the Empirical Model has advocates, it is not the only form that the appeal to intuition takes, nor the only the target of the arguments below. At least as influential is a view that treats our intuitions not as intellectual appearances, but as a subset of our ethical beliefs. The simplest picture is one of pure coherence: one's ethical beliefs are justified insofar as they belong to a system of beliefs that is simple, powerful, consistent, and explanatorily deep. The answer to the question 'Why defer to intuitions?' is not that they are akin to perceptual inputs, but that coherence is the only epistemic pressure we face: only a failure of coherence can require us to revise our initial beliefs, and what we should believe is a function of them. For David Brink, '[any] moral belief that is part of reflective equilibrium is justified according to a coherence theory of justification in ethics' (Brink 1989: 130–1). And for Geoff

Sayre-McCord, 'a person's moral beliefs are epistemically justified if, and then to the extent that, they cohere well with the other things she believes' (Sayre-McCord 1996: 176). Again, there are complications with testimony and with unjustified non-ethical beliefs; but again, they can be set aside. On the Pure Coherence View, your ethical beliefs are justified first-hand when they rest on justified non-ethical beliefs and meet permissible standards of simplicity, power, consistency, and explanatory depth.

Brink's reference to 'reflective equilibrium', in the quotation above, is an invocation of John Rawls. He, too, can be a read as a coherence theorist. But the classification is obscure.[21] First, Rawls gives special weight in reflective equilibrium to our 'considered judgements', filtered for such conditions as personal bias, unfamiliarity, and doubt. This is a minor shift. In what follows, I will count as advocates of a Pure Coherence View those who rely on coherence with a privileged class of beliefs, so long as they are not picked out by their relation to the truth.

A more substantive point is that Rawls's test for considered judgement evolved over time. Most significantly, in his 'Outline of a Decision Procedure for Ethics' (Rawls 1951: 182–3), considered judgements are confined to those on which there is general agreement, whereas, in *A Theory of Justice* he writes, memorably:

I shall not even ask whether the principles that characterize one person's considered judgments are the same as those that characterize another's.... We may suppose that everyone has in himself the whole form of a moral conception. So for the purposes of this book, the views of the reader and the author are the only ones that count. The opinions of others are used only to clear our own heads. (Rawls 1970: 50)

Consensus is not a condition on considered judgement in a Pure Coherence View.

---

[21] Important treatments of Rawls on justification include Daniels 1979 and Scanlon 2002.

Finally, and most importantly, it is not in fact clear that the procedure of reflective equilibrium is intended by Rawls as an epistemic standard, or rather as a tool for the study of 'substantive moral conceptions', with questions of truth being set aside, or a methodological proposal.[22]

Whatever Rawls himself believed, the idea of reflective equilibrium has been profoundly influential in epistemology, an influence reflected in both the Empirical Model and the Pure Coherence View, and it is the epistemological reading that will occupy us here. Between them, these views are so widespread as to count as orthodox in moral theory; here they are generalized to ethics and practical reason.[23] Despite their prevalence, I will argue that they can't be right. On the Empirical Model, we can renew the style of argument considered in section 1, from disagreement to scepticism. If we revise the model to avoid this consequence, we fall into another trap: a form of Epistemic Egoism on which we are justified in thinking that our intellectual faculties are more reliable than those of other people, when we have no evidence that it is true. A similar implication faults the Pure Coherence View.

Begin with the Empirical Model, unrevised. This model treats intuitions as evidence for ethical beliefs in much the way that perceptual appearances are evidence for beliefs about the empirical world. The problem is that, although the Equal Weight View fails, it gives the right response to perceptual disagreement. It is cases of conflicting perception that initially motivate this view. Elga gives the following example:

You and a friend are to judge the same contest, a race between Horse A and Horse B. Initially, you think that your friend is as good as you at judging such races. In other words, you think that in case of

---

[22] On substantive moral conceptions, see Rawls 1975: 7; and on methodology, Sayre-McCord 1996: 140–5.
[23] On the connection with morality in particular, and for an earlier version of the arguments to come, see 'Does Moral Theory Corrupt Youth?' (Setiya 2010b).

disagreement about the race, the two of you are equally likely to be mistaken. The race is run, and the two of you form independent judgments. As it happens, you become confident that Horse A won, and your friend becomes equally confident that Horse B won. (Elga 2007: 486)

On the most obvious way of interpreting this case, it is one in which you should become agnostic: you are no longer entitled to your belief about the winner of the race. This verdict does not depend on the Equal Weight View; it is not parochial. If we assume that you and your friend have differing perceptions, since it looks to you as though Horse A has won, while it looks the opposite way to him, the point is that your evidence has changed. Now you know how things look to your friend, you have gained evidence for the proposition that Horse B won the race; he has gained evidence that Horse A won. As Kelly points out in rejecting the Equal Weight View, 'given the relevant background assumptions and symmetries, it is natural to think that the total evidence [you] now share favors neither the proposition that Horse A finished ahead of Horse B nor the proposition that Horse B finished ahead of Horse A' (Kelly 2010: 152).

There are no doubt situations in which you should hold the line. You may have prior evidence that your perceptions are more reliable, or whatever your comparative reliability, more evidence of yours than that of your friend. You may have evidence that Horse A won the race, or that Horse B lost, apart from how things look, as perhaps what happened in earlier contests between them. There may be asymmetries of self-knowledge: it is easier to know how things look to you than to your friend.[24] But if none of these

---

[24] This qualification may explain why some resist the sceptical verdict when the disagreement is more extreme: the race does not look close to either of you; you believe that Horse A won by a length; this is what your friend believes about Horse B. Since conflicting appearances are common when a race is close, but rare when it is not, the extent of your disagreement gives you reason to doubt that things seem to your friend the way he claims they do. Once we correct for this uncertainty, the sceptical pressure returns.

conditions holds, your evidence now requires you to suspend belief. Unless you have independent reason to discount your friend's perception, you should give how things look to him as much evidential weight as how they look to you.

It follows from this point about perceptual evidence that the Empirical Model supports an inference from fundamental and intuitive disagreement to scepticism. As with the Equal Weight View, we can avoid disputes about the extent of actual disagreement by considering a hypothetical case. Suppose, once again, that you belong to a homogeneous community whose ethical beliefs are true and who are non-ethically well-informed. Let us add that your beliefs are proportioned to your intuitions, finding the perfect balance of simplicity, power, and explanatory depth, weighed against fidelity to how things seem. For the first time, you meet a stranger. He agrees with you outside of ethics, but when it comes to practical reason, his intuitions are shocking. Fill in the details as you like. Perhaps it seems to him that we should act on our final desires, whatever they are, that we should be utterly selfish, that we should maximize aggregate happiness no matter who is trampled on the way. Despite this, his ethical beliefs are as well-proportioned to his intuitions as your beliefs are to yours. It turns out that he, too, belongs to a homogenous community, exactly as numerous as your own. What should you now believe? If intuitions play the role of perceptual appearances and provide us with evidence in a similar way, the horse race argument applies. Before you meet the stranger, you have justified beliefs. But now you know how things seem to him, your confidence should fade. Apart from the intuitions in dispute, you have no basis for your ethical beliefs, and no more evidence of your reliability than his. You have no independent reason to discount the stranger's intuitions. This being so, you should give how things seem to him as much evidential weight as how they seem to you. You should thus become agnostic about the ethical questions on which you disagree.[25] As before, however, this is not the right response. We should not defer to moral monsters but condemn them, no matter how coherent or numerous they are. In disagreements of this kind, the Empirical Model gives the wrong result.

Let me stress that the argument here does not go from the possibility of fundamental, intuitive disagreement, by way of the Empirical Model, to a sceptical claim about our actual beliefs. On the Empirical Model, intuitions are epistemically akin to perceptual appearances, and while differences in how things actually seem are evidentially significant, the mere possibility that they seem different to others is not.[26] The problem is about a hypothetical case. If we were to meet both fundamental and intuitive disagreement, the Empirical Model would embrace irresolution: it would have us lose faith in ethical fact. And that is not how we should respond.

Is there any way to resist this argument? Within the strictures of the Empirical Model, there are just two moves to make. One could deny that the scenario above is really possible. Or one could dispute the application of the horse race verdict to disagreements of this more radical kind. Neither response is plausible. In considering the first, it helps to focus on a single case, that of rational egoism. The egoist believes that one should act so as to maximize net benefit to oneself. The only reason to do something is that it will be good for you. If someone holds this view, I will disagree with him about what to do in a vast array of situations: all of those in which the rights and interests of others make an ethical difference. Shocking though it is, the view in question has been held, and with apparent sincerity. The rational egoist is not impossible.

[25] For a parallel argument, see Feldman 2006: 222–4.

[26] A helpful analogy: in perceptual disagreement, we should treat the perceptual faculties of other people as if they were scientific instruments; unless we have evidence to discount them, we can assume that they are as reliable as our own. The fact that your instrument disagrees with mine is reason to become agnostic. The fact that it is possible for an instrument to disagree is not.

Nor is it impossible for him to know the facts on which the truth in ethics supervenes. He can acknowledge that others have rights and interests—or if these count as ethical truths, he can know the facts in virtue of which they hold—and yet insist that they count for nothing. Can his beliefs be fully coherent? They form a system that is simple, powerful, and explanatorily deep. Nor are they bound to run against his intuitions. Even if most of us feel bad when we see others in pain or witness injustice, and seem to ourselves to have reason to care, it is not impossible to lack these feelings or intuitions that echo them. That is how it is with our rational egoist. He rarely feels for strangers, and when he does, his feelings strike him as irrelevant. He may allow that the well-being of his close friends and family is part of his own, so that it is permissible to act on their behalf, but beyond that narrow circle, people seem to him inconsequential. Is there some hidden incoherence in this description? It is hard to see where. The coherent egoist is an ugly figure, but he is not impossible. Nor is a community of egoists, fractious and unsettled, in which life limps on from day to day, 'solitary, poor, nasty, brutish, and short' (Hobbes, *Leviathan* xiii.9).

So much for the possibility of coherent disagreement. What about the second response to the argument above? Does it matter that the disagreement between us is radical rather than mild? Consider a variant of the horse race scenario in which your friend is more wildly mistaken. Perhaps it seems to him that Horse B won because it grew wings and could fly. Here you are justified in maintaining your belief. Might the same point hold when you confront the rational egoist? No. In the horse race variation, you are justified in ignoring your friend's belief because you have independent evidence that it is false. Even apart from your present perceptions, you have evidence that horses do not grow wings and cannot fly. It is on this basis that you hold your ground. In the Empirical Model, there is no independent evidence on which to reject the intuitions of the rational egoist: the only evidence you have is the intuitions in dispute.

Finally, we can ask whether it matters that our disagreement is pervasive, not local, acknowledging the lack of independent grounds. Does the conciliatory verdict lapse when perceptual conflict is more widespread? Again, the answer is no. Although it is more difficult to imagine a pervasive clash of perceptual appearances—not just the winner of the race, but its very existence, whole stretches of experience, the deliverances of a given sense throughout one's life—if it were to obtain, this too should prompt a sceptical response. As the extent of the divergence grows, the threat to one's beliefs cannot diminish. And the basic challenge remains. How can you trust the way things seem to you, if they seem quite different to your friend, and you have no independent reason to discount his views?

Although it refutes its intended target, the present argument may continue to seem unfair. It takes the analogy between ethical intuitions and perceptual appearances seriously and asks what we should believe in perceptual disagreements of the relevant kind. The answer is that we should become agnostic. This verdict is then applied to ethical disagreements, conceived on the Empirical Model, where it gives the wrong result. Proponents of the Empirical Model may protest that they did not intend the analogy in this way. Their view is that, so long as the non-ethical beliefs on which they rest are justified, one's ethical beliefs should be proportioned to the evidence one's intuitions provide. The proportions are fixed by permissible standards of coherence and deference to how things seem. These claims say nothing about the epistemic significance of other people's intuitions, even when one has no evidence, apart from one's own intuitions, about their reliability. If we refuse to give weight, or equal weight, to the intuitions of others, we can block the inference from fundamental and intuitive disagreement to scepticism. On this reading, the analogy between ethical intuition and perceptual appearance is that each provides a basic source of evidence, not that they do so in just the same way.

The problem with this response is that, apart from distorting the analogy behind the Empirical Model, the revision leads to an unacceptable egoism, not in ethics but epistemology. The argument for this conclusion turns on a qualified 'reflection principle' for epistemic justification. To a first approximation, if S knows that he would be justified in believing p in circumstance q, he is already justified in believing the conditional, if q then p.[27] Although it is on the right track, this cannot be exactly right. We need to allow for the case in which S also knows, or has reason to believe, that his evidence in q would be misleading. This can happen in two ways. One is that q goes beyond the epistemic circumstance—the facts about S that bear on the justification of his beliefs—to indicate its unreliability. The other is that, while S now has evidence that p would not be the case in q, in circumstance q he would lose this evidence, so as to be justified in believing p. While further refinements are possible, we can work with the following claim:

REFLECTION: If S knows that he would be justified in believing p in q, where q is an epistemic circumstance that involves no relevant loss of evidence, he is already justified in believing the conditional, if q then p.

If I know that, were I to see the gauge read 2000, I would be justified in thinking that we are 2,000 feet above sea level, and this would not involve a relevant loss of evidence, I am already justified in believing that, if I see the gauge read 2000, our altitude is 2,000 feet. If I know that, were you to tell me that you are happy, I would be justified in believing you, and I would not lose any evidence I now have, I am already justified in believing that you are happy if you say you are. Matters are different if I know that the gauge is unreliable, or that you are, and that I will lose this knowledge between now and then. But if I will merely gain new evidence,

---

[27] This claim echoes White (2006: 538–9) on future justification; he also notes the need to qualify. For related though more technical discussion, see van Fraassen 1984 and Briggs 2009.

I should take the default view that justification tracks the truth: I should believe the conditional, if q then p, when I know that, in circumstance q, I would be justified in believing p.

Reflection takes us from knowledge of epistemological claims, about the justification we would have in a hypothetical circumstance, to justified beliefs about the non-epistemic world. What happens when we apply this principle to the Empirical Model, now revised? According to the revision, intuitions are unlike perceptual appearances in that we are entitled to discount each other's in the absence of independent grounds. Return to the case of fundamental, intuitive disagreement, and imagine for simplicity that you are the rational egoist I confront. If it is to save me from the sceptical inference, the Revised Empirical Model must say that I am justified in maintaining my beliefs even if, apart from the intuitions that conflict, I have no more evidence of my reliability than yours. Since the situation is symmetric, you are justified, too. Now consider the following question: what should we think about the reliability of our respective intuitions, apart from the evidence those intuitions provide? To make the question vivid, imagine that I am thinking about ethics before I have intuitions of my own, like some prodigious two-year-old epistemologist. This need not be possible, of course; the point is to focus on antecedent justification: what I am justified in thinking without appeal to intuition itself. Suppose, also, that I know the truth of the Revised Empirical Model. In particular, I know that I would be justified in sustaining the beliefs my intuitions support in fundamental, intuitive disagreement with you. This circumstance does not involve a relevant loss of evidence, since in my two-year-old state, I have none. It follows by Reflection that I am justified in believing the conditional, if we occupy the circumstance described, my beliefs are true. That is, even apart from the evidence supplied by my actual intuitions, I am justified in thinking that the ethical outlook my intuitions support is more likely to be correct than the outlook supported by yours: that my intuitions are a more reliable guide to the facts.

This consequence is intolerable. Perhaps we are entitled to trust the reliability of our perceptual and intellectual powers without the need for evidence, but not in this comparative way. On the Revised Empirical Model, I am entitled to believe that my intuitions are more reliable than yours, not on the basis of evidence but by non-evidential right. Without appeal to intuition, I can say that if our intuitions conflict, the truth corresponds to mine. Since the situation is symmetric, you can say the same about yours. Such relative confidence in our own capacities, regardless of what they tell us, amounts to Epistemic Egoism. In the absence of evidence, we are not justified in thinking that how things seem to us is a better guide to how they are than how they seem to anyone else.[28]

The Empirical Model thus confronts a dilemma. If it treats intuitions like perceptual appearances, it gives the wrong response to fundamental, intuitive disagreement. If it averts this problem by insisting on an asymmetric treatment of our own and others' intuitions, it leads to Epistemic Egoism. Revised or unrevised, the Empirical Model is false.

Does it help to reject the idea of intuitions as intellectual appearances, and to adopt instead a Pure Coherence View? On this approach, one's ethical beliefs are justified first-hand when they rest on justified non-ethical beliefs and meet permissible standards of simplicity, power, consistency, and explanatory depth. Alternatively, we privilege some subset of beliefs and appeal to coherence with them. Ignoring testimony, and assuming

---

[28] In defending something like the Revised Empirical Model, Ralph Wedgwood contends that it is rational to give more weight to my own intuitions, in part because they move me directly, while the influence of your intuitions is mediated by belief (Wedgwood 2010). At the same time, he insists that 'I have no reason to think that the mere fact that some moral intuitions are *mine* makes those intuitions any more reliable than anyone else's' (Wedgwood 2010: 239). The Reflection argument shows that one cannot combine these views.

justified non-ethical beliefs, one's degrees of ethical belief should be those that best cohere with one's considered judgements. What does this mean for the epistemology of disagreement? If my ethical beliefs are true, coherent, and non-ethically well-informed, should I be disturbed by the stranger whose beliefs are no less coherent, no less informed, but ethically appalling? On the Pure Coherence View, the answer is no. The beliefs of others do not have the epistemic standing of one's own: they count as evidence only when one has evidence of their reliability. Since that it is not so in the present case, I need not be moved by the fact that we disagree. As Sayre-McCord contends, in defence of Pure Coherence:

[Whether] one is justified in retaining one's original view in light of another depends on whether one's own evidence tells in favor of the other view or not. In the face of (even) coherent alternatives, one justifiably rejects the others, when one does, on the basis of what one justifiably believes. (Sayre-McCord 1996: 172)

By the same token, the stranger is justified in his beliefs, however shocking they are: the situation is symmetric. Since one's ethical beliefs are justified if coherent and non-ethically informed, the prospect of fundamental, coherent disagreement is epistemically harmless.

It follows that the Pure Coherence View does not share the defects of the Empirical Model in its original form. It is, however, isomorphic to the Revised Empirical Model, and like that model, it blocks the sceptical inference at the cost of Epistemic Egoism. Recall the qualified reflection principle:

REFLECTION: If S knows that he would be justified in believing p in q, where q is an epistemic circumstance that involves no relevant loss of evidence, he is already justified in believing the conditional, if q then p.

As before, we focus on antecedent justification. What should I think about the reliability of our respective beliefs, apart from the support my actual beliefs provide? Again, to make the question vivid, imagine that I am asking it before I have beliefs about the content of ethics. If I know the truth of the Pure Coherence View, I know that I would be justified in maintaining my beliefs, so long as they are coherent and well-informed, even if I know that yours are very different from mine and, apart from the issues in dispute, I have no more evidence of my reliability than yours. This circumstance does not involve a relevant loss of evidence, since in my two-year-old state, I have none. It follows by Reflection that I am justified in believing the conditional, if we occupy the circumstance described, my beliefs are true. That is, even without the support of my actual beliefs, I am justified in thinking that the ethical outlook my beliefs support is more likely to be correct than the outlook supported by yours: that my beliefs are a more reliable guide to the ethical facts. Since the situation is symmetric, you should think the same about yours. We are each entitled to believe that our own intellectual faculties are more reliable, not on the basis of evidence but by non-evidential right. We have been led from Pure Coherence to Epistemic Egoism.

I end this section by answering two questions. First: the charge of egoism implies an unacceptable bias towards oneself; does that go beyond what the argument shows? It is true that, on the Pure Coherence View, I am non-evidentially justified in thinking that my beliefs are more reliable than yours, where they turn out to conflict. This looks like an egocentric bias. What if we insist, however, that justification is permissive, and that I am equally justified in thinking that your beliefs are more reliable than mine? Both attitudes are epistemically rational. I am permitted to believe that I would get things right, if we were to disagree, and I am permitted to believe the same about you. I am not required to favour my own beliefs.

There are two problems with this response. One is that permission is bad enough, even if it goes both ways. I am not entitled to believe that my intellectual faculties are more reliable than yours, in the absence of evidence; to add that I am also permitted to believe the opposite does not affect this. The permissive reading of Pure Coherence is in any case flawed. We can see this by thinking about Reflection. In effect, Reflection is a principle of transmission on which knowledge of the epistemic status p would have in q transmits that status to the conditional, if q then p. It follows that we can take a permissive view of my attitude to this conditional only if we take an equally permissive view of the attitude I should have when we disagree. We would have to say that I am justified in maintaining my beliefs in coherent, fundamental disagreement only in that I am permitted to do so, where I am also permitted to revise those beliefs and adopt yours instead. If you believe that we should be utterly selfish and I deny it, the epistemic status of our positions is, from my point of view, the same: they are equally worthy of belief. Though it is not exactly sceptical, this consequence is one we should hope to avoid. Properly conceived, the Pure Coherence View avoids it. It holds that when we disagree in fundamental but coherent ways, each of us is justified in our beliefs, meaning that we should maintain them in the face of conflict: it would not be rational to give them up. It is this bias in favour of what we happen to believe that Reflection transmutes into Epistemic Egoism.

The second question is how my argument differs from the standard complaint that coherence theories fail to connect justification with truth. The answer lies in a contrast already drawn, between the proposition that our basic faculties are reliable and the proposition that ours are more reliable than others' when their outputs diverge. A principle of interpretive charity on which beliefs are by nature true, although defeasibly so, or on which they tend to count as knowledge, might begin to explain their reliability.[29] It might give a priori grounds for trust in our

---

[29] For versions of this idea, see, especially, Davidson 1983: 146–51 and Williamson 2007: Ch. 8.

perceptual and intellectual faculties. In doing so, it would help to dissolve the standard objection to epistemologies of pure coherence. It would, however, do nothing at all to explain how we are justified in thinking that our intellectual faculties are more reliable than those of other people when we have no evidence that it is true. The principle of charity is not in this way comparative or egoistic.

To summarize our conclusions. In its original form, the Empirical Model warrants the inference from fundamental and intuitive disagreement to scepticism. In resisting this inference, we must reject or revise that model. If we do so by refusing to give weight, or equal weight, to the intuitions of others, we are compelled by Reflection to Epistemic Egoism. Since the implication is false, so is the Revised Empirical Model. Nor does it help to replace intuitions as appearances with a subset of beliefs, as in the Pure Coherence View. For the egoistic consequence remains. None of these views accounts for the justification of ethical belief.

3. BIAS TOWARDS THE TRUTH

The immediate question is: what alternative do we have? The strategy of beginning with what we believe, or what seems true to us, can strike one as inevitable. And in a sense, it is. The mistake is to confuse this methodological point with one in epistemology. That we must begin inquiry with our own beliefs, revising and improving them as we can, is not to say that, if we make our beliefs coherent with our intuitions, they are epistemically justified.

If not coherence or intuition, what justifies ethical beliefs? One answer is testimony. We may be told what is right and wrong, or what there is reason to do. Some find this prospect disturbing or problematic.[30] And it gives at best a partial view. In learning from testimony, one's belief inherits its justification from that of one's informant. She might have been told by someone else; but eventually the regress ends. If ethical beliefs are justified, some are justified first-hand.[31]

In asking how they are justified, we will thus ignore the role of ethical testimony. We will also adopt the mild evidentialism that served as the backdrop to the Empirical Model. One's degrees of belief should be proportioned to one's evidence, where one's evidence consists in a set of propositions or attitudes to which one bears some special relation. This view may seem disputably 'foundationalist', but once we reject epistemologies of Pure Coherence, as we did in section 2, it is difficult to resist. The picture is extremely non-committal: it allows for justified beliefs that need no grounds; nor does it much constrain the nature of evidence and evidential support. Still, within its flexible frame we can articulate possible structures of justification in ethics. When they are justified, do ethical beliefs rest on evidence? And if they do, what could this evidence be?

I will argue that the basic evidence for ethical claims is not itself ethical: our evidence lies in the facts on which the truth in ethics supervenes, or in non-ethical evidence that those facts obtain. I will approach this view by considering, first, the appeal to self-evidence or non-evidential justification; and then the appeal to evidence whose content is ethical. I then return to the problem of disagreement, showing how to avoid both Epistemic Egoism and the sceptical inference. The key is to recognize that basic

---

[30] For a defence of moral knowledge by testimony, see Jones 1999; and for accounts of what is odd about it, see Nickel 2001; Driver 2006; Hopkins 2007; Hills 2009; McGrath 2009, 2011.

[31] It is possible to miss this point if one thinks of moral education as, in general, a matter of testimony. But this conflation is a mistake. Learning right from wrong is learning to distinguish them oneself, not to take the distinction on trust.

standards of justification in ethics are biased towards the truth. The explanation and defence of this idea—an account of how evidence relates to belief when ethical belief is justified or when it counts as knowledge—will occupy the next three chapters of the book.

What would it mean to think of ethical beliefs as epistemically justified not on the basis of evidence? Some philosophers refuse to speak of 'evidence' here at all. It sounds odd to cite my intuitions, or the facts of what you did, as evidence that you acted well. But this is a matter of words. We are to understand evidence in the abstract terms set out above: as a set of propositions or attitudes to which one bears some special relation, and to which one's degrees of belief should be proportioned. When one's belief is justified by some attitude one has, or by the content of that attitude, it rests on evidence in our abstract sense.[32] If ethical beliefs are non-evidentially justified, their justification does not turn on intuitions, appearances, beliefs, or anything of the kind.

The idea that ethical beliefs are non-evidentially justified is a form of intuitionism that might also be expressed with the language of 'self-evidence'.[33] I avoid this term because it wrongly suggests that the content of these beliefs 'when made explicit ... must be accepted at once by an intelligent and unbiased mind' (Sidgwick 1907: 229). This form of psychological compulsion does not follow from the claim that some of us are justified in believing things without evidential support. When your belief that

---

[32] A qualification: when one should believe p on the basis of evidence, anyone who shares that evidence should believe it, too. Evidential support is in this way 'objective': it fixes epistemic probability. This fact explains how self-knowledge can be groundless even though it depends on our mental states. If I am justified in self-ascribing belief in p partly because I believe p, I am justified by a propositional attitude. It does not follow that I am justified by evidence, since the attitude in question would not justify others in ascribing the belief to me. This complication is irrelevant to the arguments in the text.

[33] As in Ross 1930: 29; Shafer-Landau 2003: 247; Audi 2004: 48–9.

p is non-evidentially justified, I may yet deny that *p*. Clear-headed disagreement is possible.[34]

Even 'intuitionism' could mislead. According to a standard definition, the intuitionist holds that 'we possess some genuinely non-inferential ethical knowledge' (Sturgeon 2002: 187) or that 'some basic moral truths are non-inferentially known' (Audi 2004: 5). This formulation runs together justification without evidence and justification by evidence but not by inference from other beliefs.[35] On the Empirical Model, our evidence consists in intuitions as intellectual appearances. If we form beliefs on the basis of our intuitions, unmediated by other beliefs, we might arrive at knowledge without inference. By the standard definition, this counts as intuitionism, though it is quite different from a non-evidential view.[36]

The difference is significant. In a recent critique of intuitionism, Walter Sinnott-Armstrong argues that knowledge of disagreement undermines non-inferentially justified beliefs. He begins with perception as a paradigm of non-inferential knowledge. Considering a case in which things look different to each of us, he argues that, 'if I have no reason to believe that my visual identifications are more reliable than yours, I am not justified in trusting mine after I learn that you disagree with me' (Sinnott-Armstrong 2002: 312). This matches our verdict about perceptual disagreement and the Empirical Model in section 2. Sinnott-Armstrong claims, however, that the point is general:[37]

---

[34] A point that has been emphasized by others (Shafer-Landau 2003: 256–8, 261–3; Audi 2004: 53–4).

[35] Here, as elsewhere in this section, I ignore the distinction between knowledge and justified belief; nothing I say depends on it. Where the distinction is significant, it will be made explicit.

[36] Defenders of self-evidence sometimes confuse their view with the Empirical Model, as when Ross calls 'the moral convictions of thoughtful and well-educated people . . . the data of ethics' and compares them to 'sense-perceptions [as] the data of natural science' (Ross 1930: 41). See also Audi on the 'evidential weight' of intuitions, including 'the apparent intuitions of *others*' (Audi 2004: 47).

[37] See also Doris and Plakias 2008: 309–10; McGrath 2008: §6.

If I know that others hold beliefs contrary to mine, then I need to be able to draw some kind of inference to support my belief or undermine theirs before I can be justified in believing that I am correct and they are incorrect. In short, disagreement creates a need for inferential justification. (Sinnott-Armstrong 2002: 312)

The problem is that what holds for one sort of knowledge without inference, the kind that rests on appearances as evidence, need not hold for others. In perceptual disagreement, our prior situation is symmetric: our beliefs are justified by how things seem. Since we have no independent reason to discount each other's perceptions, our post-confrontation evidence is shared: it favours suspension of belief. (This is what happened in the horse race scenario.) If you are to hold your ground in the face of this, you need some other source of justification, perhaps by inference from other beliefs. By contrast, non-evidential justification may be asymmetric all along. If your prior belief is justified, though not by evidence, and my belief lacks all support, this disparity survives our disagreement. I should never have believed what I did. Nor should you be strongly moved by what I think. The fact of dissent is not enough to tip the epistemic balance.[38]

We will return to disagreement below. For now, the point is to distinguish intuitions as evidence in the Empirical Model from the non-evidential view, even if both permit non-inferentially justified belief. If we conflate these views, we risk finding objections to one conclusive against the other—when they are not.

---

[38] This point echoes the objection to Equal Weight described in section 1. In generalizing from perception, Sinnott-Armstrong cites an example of mathematical disagreement in which the sceptical verdict seems right (Sinnott-Armstrong 2002: 314). The case he considers is, however, one of belief without explicit inference, about the answer to an SAT question, not belief without evidence, and therefore does not speak to the argument in the text. A more relevant example might be one in which we disagree about the proposition that 2 plus 2 is 5. (This may be impossible; if so, insert the most outrageous mathematical claim you think could be endorsed.) If my belief is non-evidentially justified and yours is not, I should not become agnostic when I learn of your dissent.

The idea of knowledge without evidence is often associated with knowledge of necessary truths. At the very least, one cannot know that a particular act or agent falls under an ethical concept, E, without having evidence of any kind. What we know without evidence is general: if x is N then x is E. We combine this with knowledge that some particular x is N to draw an ethical conclusion, x is E.

This picture raises various questions. What are the conditions of non-evidential support? Is it that certain propositions are privileged, presumably true ones, and that it is sufficient to believe them with justification that one believe them at all? Should we further require the absence of defeating evidence? Or that one's belief be explained by 'adequate understanding'?[39] What does that involve? In fact, however, there is a more pressing objection to confront. Take the judgement that an act is wrong. While it often rests on beliefs whose content is not ethical, together with belief in a relevant conditional, the conditional believed is not a necessary truth.[40] Even detailed accounts of the circumstance of action, non-ethically described, leave room for countervailing reasons, facts consistent with the circumstance that would make an ethical difference. If I think you acted wrongly in hitting that child, there are countless ways the world could be, most of them unimagined by me, that would justify what you did. Perhaps you hit her in order to kill the lethal insect on her arm. Perhaps you acted under threat. Perhaps she will feel no pain. While I readily cite non-ethical facts as grounds for my belief—the child is young; you hit her hard—they fail to necessitate its truth. Asked to supplement these facts to fix the entailment, I am at a loss. There are too many loopholes to close.

In saying this, I do not assume the falsehood of hedonistic utilitarianism, on which the facts that entail an ethical judgement

---

[39] As in Audi 2004: 48–51.
[40] This argument has been made by Sarah McGrath (2004: 218–19).

are simple, not complex, or of other views that share this property—though I do not find them plausible. What I assume is that those, like me, who reject such views are not deprived of ethical knowledge. When I know the worth of an act or agent, that it is right or wrong, that she is generous or unjust, I can rarely give non-ethical grounds sufficient to entail what I believe. The grounds I could supply allow for defeating conditions of many kinds, and while I doubt that such conditions obtain, that is itself an ethical stance. That nothing undermines my claim about the worth of this act, or this agent, is not a premise for deduction from non-ethical facts.

Typically, then, when I know that x is E by way of the conditional, if x is N then x is E, the conditional is a contingent truth. Nor is it something I am entitled to believe without evidence. This is not to say that contingent claims can never be justified in that way. The thought that they can—that we are non-evidentially entitled to some contingent truths—is part of one response to perceptual and inductive scepticism.[41] The propositions in question there, however, are more or less abstract, concerning the uniformity of nature or the reliability of appearance. The conditionals we cite in ethical judgement are not of this kind. The possibilities in which they are false are ones in which x is N but not E, as when you hit the child but act permissibly, killing the lethal insect on her arm. These possibilities are ones I can exclude only with cause—as, for instance, evidence that there was no insect or that lethal insects are rare. If I am justified in believing the conditional despite the prospect of defeating conditions, I am justified by evidence that they do not obtain.

It might be argued, against the line I am taking here, that when I believe a conditional with non-ethical antecedent and ethical consequent, I implicitly believe the logically weaker conditional obtained by strengthening the antecedent to make a necessary

[41] See Cohen 1999, 2010; White 2006; and, with qualifications, Wright 2004.

truth. But this is barely plausible—I may not have the concepts required so much as to think this antecedent; nor does it play a role in my psychic life—and even if true, it would not save the deductive view. It is essential to this view not only that I believe the necessary conditional, but that I do so without evidence. If I believe it only as a consequence of something stronger, a contingent claim for which I have grounds, then this condition fails.

Let me stress that my argument is not about the possibility of non-evidential justification, either in principle or in practice. Given adequate self-knowledge, non-ethical data, and reflective power, perhaps one could deduce that an act is right from a conditional known without evidence. As we will see in chapter two, the view that I defend makes room for this. The point I am making now is that we do not usually manage it, and that we need not do so in order to be justified in our beliefs. Likewise, we may have non-evidential knowledge of pro tanto reasons, as perhaps that there is always reason to avoid harm.[42] But such beliefs are not sufficient, together with the application of non-ethical concepts, to deduce that an act is wrong.

According to the argument so far, beliefs about the worth of an act or agent are evidentially justified, when they are justified at all; but the relation of evidence to belief is not deductive. We do not typically know that an act is right or wrong, an agent generous or unjust, by deducing this from claims that we know without evidence, along with non-ethical facts. How, then, does evidence support our ethical beliefs? On what basis do we know contingent facts about the application of ethical concepts?

In general, one's evidence consists in a set of propositions or attitudes to which one bears some special relation, and to which one's degrees of belief should be proportioned. We can ask, then,

---

[42] This idea is due to Ross on 'prima facie duties' (Ross 1930). It is shared by recent intuitionists (Shafer-Landau 2003: Ch. 11; Audi 2004), who give other accounts of 'verdictive belief'.

whether the evidence that supports a belief about the worth of an act or agent is ethical or not. Does it involve an attitude whose content involves the application of an ethical concept? Or is it that the act or agent falls under non-ethical concepts, N?

The arguments of section 2 give us reason to doubt that the evidence is ethical. If it is supplied by ethical intuitions, either as appearances or initial beliefs, we end up with the Empirical Model or the Pure Coherence View. Nor can we fruitfully appeal to knowledge as evidence.[43] For we can still ask how, or on what grounds, an ethical proposition is known. Barring circularity or regress, we must eventually appeal to another source of evidence, ethical or not, or to no evidence at all.

An option that remains is to invoke as evidence only veridical intuitions.[44] On this conception, the sceptical inference that marred the Empirical Model may not go through. When your prior belief is justified, since you perceive the truth, and my belief lacks all support, our situation is epistemically asymmetric. This asymmetry may survive our dissent, leaving your belief justified, as mine never was. My objection to this idea is not that it is impossible, but that its scope is limited. In the typical case, ethical perception of an act or agent is not immediate; it rests on evidence about the non-ethical character of its object.[45] What did she do, to whom, and why? We need not be able to articulate this evidence in full or to explain its relevance. And, as we have seen, our evidence may not entail the ethical verdict it supports. Still, it does vital epistemic work. One way to bring this out is to stress how commonly we reflect on situations that we do not occupy, as when they are merely described to us, or when we plan for possible futures. The circumstance at hand is specified in ways that do not beg the ethical question: the description on the basis

---

[43] As in Williamson 2000: Ch. 8.

[44] This is a form of 'epistemic disjunctivism'; see McDowell 2008.

[45] For a similar claim, see Zimmerman 2010: 84–6; and in defence of immediacy, Johnston 2001, McGrath 2004, and Dancy 2010.

of which we make an ethical judgement is not itself ethical. Still, we form justified beliefs about the act or agent that the circumstance involves. If intuition plays a role here, it is derivative, at best: it mediates between non-ethical evidence and ethical judgement. Both judgement and intuition have non-ethical grounds. For the most part, this is true even when an intuition is caused by the situation it is about. When something strikes me as kind or contemptuous, it does so on the basis of other representations, ones whose content is ethically indifferent. Again, I may not be able to cite or describe these representations, except to say that there was something about his action or expression that struck me this way. But the representations are epistemically engaged.

What I am urging, then, is not that we have no ethical evidence, but that it does not account for much of what we know. What can be thought of as the paradigm of ethical judgement is judgement not on the basis of immediate intuition, but of non-ethical fact. This is paradigmatic in part because we cannot do without it; in part because, once we have it, it is all we need. In this respect, it differs from non-evidentially justified belief, and from belief on the basis of immediate intuition, each of which saves a fragment of ethical knowledge, while neither explains the greater part. Even if they are possible, these modes of justification are too narrow; and with the capacity for judgement, they are not required.

It is for this reason that I focus on ethical beliefs that are justified by evidence, in our abstract sense, and for which the evidence is non-ethical. This is a posteriori justification, in that the evidence in question is empirical. If there is a priori knowledge of contingent facts, it is not of the facts on which ethical judgement rests. It does not follow, however, that evidence supports ethical judgement in anything like the way it supports a posteriori knowledge elsewhere. In particular, we should not think of the relation between non-ethical evidence and ethical judgement, where the judgement is epistemically justified, as one of induction or inference to the best explanation. Induction looks obviously irrelevant. And even if ethical facts explain non-ethical effects, as some have urged,[46] it is not by reference to those effects that our beliefs are typically justified. Most often, when we know an ethical fact, we have little idea what it explains, if it explains anything at all.[47]

A more promising view would treat the facts in virtue of which an ethical concept is instantiated, or evidence of those facts, as evidence of its instantiation. The context for this proposal is a claim discussed in the introduction and relied on at various points above:

ETHICAL SUPERVENIENCE: If an act or agent falls under ethical concept, E, it does so in virtue of falling under non-ethical concepts, N, such that necessarily, what falls under N falls under E.

What is the evidence by which I am justified in believing that an act is right or wrong, an agent generous or unjust? It is evidence that the act or agent falls under non-ethical concepts, N, where, necessarily, what falls under N is right or wrong, generous or unjust. Call this Reductive Epistemology, since it reduces evidence in ethics to evidence elsewhere.

Some clarifications. First, the evidence in question is simply evidence that the act or agent falls under N. It is not evidence for the conditional, if x is N then x is E, but for its antecedent. Its being evidence that x is N is a matter of non-ethical epistemology: hence 'reductive'. What the present view adds is that evidence for the proposition that x is N counts as evidence that x is E when, in virtue of being N, an object is or would be E. If it is wrong to cause

---

[46] Notably, Sturgeon 1988.

[47] This point is emphasized in McGrath 2004: 214–15. Having argued that knowledge of particular moral facts cannot rest on deduction from necessary truths, or on inference to the best explanation, McGrath is led to the moral perception view. As I have argued, this view is too limited to explain very much of what we know. McGrath's argument goes wrong by ignoring the possibility I explore: non-ethical evidence supports our beliefs, though not by deduction or by the methods involved in a posteriori knowledge of non-ethical fact. (This possibility is absent, too, from a later essay on moral disagreement; see, especially, McGrath 2008: 102–3.)

pain for one's own enjoyment, evidence that I hurt you for fun is evidence that I acted wrongly.

Second, that my belief is justified by evidence of this kind is not to say that I grasp the concepts, N, or that I believe that, necessarily, what falls under N is right or wrong, generous or unjust. The model is not deductive. Nor does it follow that I can specify the evidence that justifies my belief. When we make an ethical judgement, we often appeal to facts, or putative facts, about an act or agent. So, for instance, I think you acted wrongly because you hit a child, because she was young, because you hit her hard. These are facts I can cite as evidence for my ethical claim. But, as we saw above, the conditional that connects these facts to the claim that you acted wrongly is contingent, and if it is justified, it rests on evidence, too. Although I have it, this further evidence may go beyond what I could cite or what figures in the content of my beliefs.[48]

Third, it is no part of Reductive Epistemology that the evidence will be dialectically useful or sufficient to persuade those who disagree. Repeating the facts of the case may well be ineffective. But as we know from the figure of the sceptic, dialectical efficacy is not a condition of evidential support.[49]

Finally, and most importantly, there is no suggestion that having evidence that an act falls under N, or believing that it is right or wrong on the basis of such evidence, is sufficient by itself to justify one's belief. In general, there is a gap between having evidence for a proposition and believing it with justification. In order to be

---

[48] Here I deny a principle of antecedent justification: if you are justified in believing p by evidence q, you must believe the conditional, if q then p, on other grounds. This denial was implicit in my discussion of the non-evidential view. It is consistent with a demand for antecedent 'propositional' justification: that you are entitled to believe the conditional, if q then p, without appeal to evidence q. Roger White defends this requirement against one form of 'dogmatism' in epistemology. See White 2006 on Pryor 2000, 2004; and for complications, Weatherson 2007. These issues are pursued in chapter two.

[49] Again, this is a topic of chapter two.

justified, one's belief must relate to that evidence in the right way. The question we have been asking is: what evidence, if any, is required for first-hand ethical knowledge? Having answered that question, we can still ask how and when this evidence plays its justifying role. That is what we will do, at length, in the later chapters of this book. What we can say now is that the further conditions of justification do not involve the possession of evidence, but the relation of evidence to justified belief.[50]

Having sketched the reductive view, it may be useful to repeat and elaborate our example. In the case described above, I think you acted wrongly in hitting a child. If I am asked to justify this belief, I can cite non-ethical grounds: the child was young, you hit her hard. But the grounds I cite do not entail that my belief is true. There are many possible worlds in which you hit a young child hard but act permissibly in doing so. What is more, these possibilities are ones that I need evidence to ignore. Did you hit the child in order to kill the lethal insect on her arm? Were you threatened in some terrible way? Is she unable to feel pain? That I am entitled to discount these prospects is a function of further evidence, not of non-evidential right. On grounds too complex to articulate, I am entitled to doubt that there is a lethal insect on the child's arm, that someone has threatened to kill the child, or her family, unless you hit her hard, that she is under anaesthetic—and a host of other claims that would make an ethical difference. I need not have considered these claims, but my evidence counts against them. It is this whole array of evidence, not just the facts I cite, that justifies my belief. Even taken in full, my evidence need not entail that you acted wrongly. What must be true is that there is an intricate

---

[50] Is there room for a hybrid view on which intuitions count as evidence, too? In principle, yes; but in practice, it is hard to make out. Veridical intuitions more plausibly mediate between non-ethical evidence and ethical belief; they do not provide us with evidence of their own. Non-veridical intuitions are relevant to 'non-ideal theory', which evaluates subjects for whom justification and apparent truth diverge.

non-ethical claim, that your act was N, by which my ethical verdict is entailed, and that, as a matter of non-ethical epistemology, my evidence makes it likely that your act was N.[51]

Though there is evidently more to say, even this partial epistemology for ethics is enough to solve the problem of ethical disagreement. The puzzle was how to block the inference from fundamental disagreement to scepticism without embracing an epistemically egoistic view. The answer is that, in disagreements of this kind, the beliefs of those who are in the right are not only true but what the evidence supports. When they meet a stranger who believes that we should act on our final desires, whatever they are, that we should be utterly selfish, that we should maximize aggregate happiness, no matter who is trampled on the way, their epistemic situation is asymmetric. The stranger's beliefs are not only false, but go against the evidence—non-ethical descriptions of the world—on which both sides agree. He should never have believed what he did, nor should the wise be strongly moved by his dissent.

This is not a matter of Epistemic Egoism, but of bias towards the truth. For the egoist, the situation is symmetric: each disputant should believe that he is more reliable. In a Reductive Epistemology, symmetry fails. The stranger is not permitted to favour his own beliefs: he should defer to the evidence that refutes them. And those whose beliefs are true have evidence that they are getting things right.

That justification is biased towards the truth is common ground among non-egoistic, non-concessive views. It is shared

---

[51] Two things distinguish this account from that of Aaron Zimmerman (2010: Ch. 5), with which it can otherwise be compared. First, he focuses on inference from beliefs, where I allow for evidence of other kinds. One's evidence may derive from attitudes, like perceptual seemings, that are not beliefs. Second, he concentrates on the deductive case, in which one's inference is informally valid: it is impossible for its premise to be true and its conclusion false. Although I think it happens, I believe that this case is rare: most ethical judgements rest on inconclusive grounds. For suggestions of this more flexible view, see Zimmerman 2010: 123.

with non-evidential intuitionism and with the appeal to veridical intuitions as evidence. In each case, the epistemic position of those who believe the truth is stronger than that of those who do not. True beliefs can be justified without evidence or by perception of the facts. Although I complained of their limitations, these models agree on the basic point, that we must break the symmetry of disagreement in favour of truth.

It does not follow from this that, if our beliefs are true, and we are justified in holding them, we should be utterly dogmatic. It may be rational for us to doubt our own reliability, perhaps on the basis of inconsistencies or past mistakes, or when we have reason to trust the opinions of those with whom we disagree. What matters for our discussion is that, if the standards of epistemology in ethics are biased towards the truth, there is no path from fundamental disagreement to scepticism: there is room to discount the opinions of others, when we should.

Although it is not a counsel of unreflectiveness or solipsism, Reductive Epistemology makes the standards of justification for ethical belief 'internal to ethics'.[52] This claim is easy to read in ways that make it seem implausible or banal: as endorsing Pure Coherence, as conflating moral and epistemic reasons, or as reminding us that reflection must begin with what we think.[53] The substantive truth in the vicinity is that ethical education is education not only into the space of practical reasons but into the space of reasons for and against our ethical beliefs. As John McDowell writes:

[52] Dworkin 1996 gives trenchant expression to this idea; see also McDowell 1998, Part II.

[53] Dworkin (1996: 117–20) comes close to the first mistake in his stubborn response to scepticism, and to the second at various points; see Dworkin 1996: 98, 122, 125. McDowell's invocations of Neurath on repairing the ship at sea (e.g. at McDowell 1994: 80–2 or McDowell 1995a: 188–9) can easily suggest epistemologies of Pure Coherence, or the boring fact that we must start with our own beliefs.

Ethical thinking is local in two ways: first, its characteristic concepts are not intelligible independently of particular cultural perspectives; and, second, it aims (explicitly or implicitly) to be directed by standards of good and bad argument, and the standards available to it are not independent of its own substantive and disputable conclusions. (McDowell 1986: 380)

What counts as evidence in ethics is evidence for the facts in virtue of which an ethical proposition is, or would be, true. The conditionals involved in Supervenience thus constrain epistemology. Against the Empirical Model and the Pure Coherence View, we cannot divorce the justification of ethical belief from the standards of ethics those conditionals encode. We cannot extricate facts about right and wrong, virtue and vice, from facts about the evidence for their truth.

A consequence of this account is that the epistemology of ethics is no more accessible to us than ethics itself. This can be disconcerting, but it is, I think, inevitable. When we meet the consistent stranger, we have no way to assess the justification of his beliefs that is independent of whether they are true. This prompts a partial concession to the Pure Coherence View. Since we must rely on our ethical beliefs not only as a guide to ethics but to its epistemology, an egoistic trust in those beliefs may be impossible to avoid. If we accept a Reductive Epistemology then, whatever we believe, we will take the evidence to be on our side. If the stranger's beliefs are unjustified, that is not something he can see, and in aspiring to conform to the standards of epistemic justification, he will be led to maintain his views. What else could we expect him to do? The stranger's intransigence is epistemically blameless, and in that weak sense justified, even when it leads him astray. In fundamental disagreement, epistemic blamelessness may be symmetric, while the support of evidence is not.

This book is concerned with epistemic standings that go beyond mere blamelessness: with knowledge, evidence, and what we should believe. I have argued that epistemic justification in ethics is biased towards the truth. More specifically, we should count as evidence for an ethical proposition evidence for the facts in virtue of which that proposition is, or would be, true. To this extent, the epistemology of ethics is itself an ethical subject. But only to this extent. Nothing I have said so far precludes 'external' challenges to ethical belief. The problem of disagreement is solved, but others remain. These sceptical problems must draw on defeating conditions other than disagreement, on objections to Reductive Epistemology, or on conditions of knowledge or justification that go beyond sufficient evidence. In what follows, I confront the most compelling arguments of this kind: from the threat of coincidence to reliability, and of accidentally true belief. In doing so, I complete the epistemological picture partly sketched so far. How does non-ethical evidence do its epistemic work? And what more is involved in ethical knowledge than having evidence for the truth of one's belief?

2

Reliability

According to the Reductive Epistemology of chapter one, ethical knowledge ordinarily rests on evidence, evidence for non-ethical facts in virtue of which an ethical proposition is, or would be, true. The proposition known is not deduced from a conditional, if x is N then x is E, belief in which is non-evidentially justified. The relation of ethical knowledge to evidence is more direct.

The argument for this position turned on the defects of the Empirical Model and the Pure Coherence View, and on the limited scope of testimony, non-evidential justification, and ethical evidence in explaining what we know. In making this argument, I did not consider objections, and I left the story of justification schematic at best. We have an answer to the question, what evidence justifies our beliefs? We have no clear picture of when, or how.

It will take some time for that picture to emerge in full: it will not be complete until the end of the book. This chapter takes preliminary steps. Section 1 replies to the objection that, in order to be justified in believing p by evidence q one must be antecedently justified in believing the conditional, if q then p. This principle threatens Reductive Epistemology by blocking the inference to an ethical conclusion from non-ethical premises, or evidence, alone. The response contrasts doxastic and propositional justification for conditionals that relate one's evidence to ethical belief. The latter may be antecedently required; the former is not. What, then, are the conditions of justification? I argue that a form of reliability is necessary, if not sufficient, for knowledge on the basis of evidence, and trace the consequent entanglement of ethical and ordinary wisdom.

This sets the stage for the rest of the chapter, which treats the sceptical argument from coincidence. Can we take ourselves to be reliable if our reliability would be an inexplicable fact? And if we doubt our own reliability, can we persist in our beliefs? For some, these questions place constraints on the nature of ethics, undermining 'ethical realism'.[1] In sections 2 and 3, I contest this view, explaining how belief in one's reliability is or can be justified, regardless of realism, and without illicit question-begging. The problem of coincidence is a myth.

1. ETHICAL JUDGEMENT

In the *Treatise of Human Nature*, Hume complained that

In every system of morality, which I have hitherto met with . . . the author proceeds for some time in the ordinary ways of reasoning, and establishes the being of a God, or makes observations concerning human affairs; when all of a sudden I am surpriz'd to find, that instead of the usual copulations of propositions, *is*, and *is not*, I meet with no proposition that is not connected with an *ought*, or an *ought not*. This change is imperceptible; but is however, of the last consequence. For as this *ought*, or *ought not*, expresses some new relation or affirmation, 'tis necessary that it shou'd be observ'd and explain'd; and at the same time that a reason shou'd be given; for what seems altogether inconceivable, how this new relation can be a deduction from others, which are entirely different from it. (Hume, *Treatise* 3.1.1.27)

'Deduction' here means inference of any kind.[2] Hume's challenge thus applies to Reductive Epistemology, which seems to permit the move from x is N to x is E without the need for any ethical

---

[1] Street 2006, ms.; using arguments in the spirit of Field 1989: 25–30, 230–9.
[2] See Owen 1999.

premise. Hume does not say that such inference is bound to be unreasonable, but its rationality must be explained.

Moore took a related view: 'To hold that from any proposition asserting "Reality is of this nature" we can infer, or obtain confirmation for, any proposition asserting "This is good in itself" is to commit the naturalistic fallacy' (Moore 1903: §67).[3] If I am justified in believing that x is E on the ground that x is N, the conditional, if x is N then x is E, must be an analytic truth. This is possible only if E can be analysed in terms of N, which Moore notoriously denied.

As a principle of evidence, as such, Moore's claim is quite implausible. There is no reason to suppose that every path from evidence to belief outside of ethics rests on analytic truths of the kind that he invokes—confirmation theory need not be analytic— and no reason to believe that ethics is in this way special.[4] Reductive Epistemology does not imply or presuppose the kind of analytic reductionism on which the meaning of ethical concepts can be specified in non-ethical terms.

The most that could be claimed on Moore's behalf is that, when beliefs are justified by evidence, there is a connection between evidence and belief that goes beyond *being evidence for*. In order to be justified in believing p by evidence q one must be antecedently justified in believing the conditional, if q then p. As we will see, this principle is crucially ambiguous. On one reading, it implies 'what is often called the autonomy of ethics: the thesis that from entirely nonethical premises there is no reasonable inference to any ethical conclusion' (Sturgeon 2002: 190). As Nicholas Sturgeon notes, the principle of autonomy can be generalized to other ' "divides" that have animated philosophers' skeptical worries' (Sturgeon 2002: 200). For Sturgeon, 'there is no reasonable inference to any conclusion about unobservables from premises that are entirely

---

[3] See also Moore 1903: §86.
[4] This point is emphasized in Sturgeon 2002: 196.

about observables' (Sturgeon 2002: 201). Generalizing further, we reach the following claim:

In order to be justified in believing p by evidence q, one must believe the conditional, if q then p, and be justified in doing so without appeal to q.

This principle conflicts with Reductive Epistemology, on which ethical beliefs are justified by non-ethical evidence without the need for any belief that connects the two. Of course, we sometimes believe that x is E on the basis of a conditional, if x is N then x is E. In the example from chapter one, I think you acted wrongly because you hit a child, because she was young, because you hit her hard. But my belief in the conditional, if you did these things, you acted wrongly, itself depends on evidence, q, which I am unable to cite. If I believe the conditional, if q and you did these things, you acted wrongly, I do so in virtue of the simpler belief, that if you did these things, you acted wrongly, which rests on q. If my beliefs are justified, they violate the principle above.

My response is to dispute the principle. One objection cites perceptual evidence, which derives from how things look or sound or feel, not from beliefs whose contents play the role of q. When I know things on the basis of experience, must I have beliefs about the experience by which I am justified? Does the principle say otherwise? But we need not press this point. Even when we believe on the basis of evidence supplied by other beliefs, our grounds may be incredibly complex. As Gilbert Harman writes, '[it] is doubtful that anyone has ever fully specified an actual piece of inductive reasoning, since it is unlikely that anyone could specify the relevant total evidence in any actual case' (Harman 1973: 28–9). Harman's claim is that we cannot articulate the evidence by which we have been influenced in full. My claim is stronger: that its influence need not be mediated by a conditional belief whose antecedent gives our total evidence and whose consequent is the conclusion we draw. The work of evidence in one's thinking need not take this deductive form.

What lies behind the demand for antecedently justified belief? Not, so far as I know, a convincing argument. It may derive from a tendency to conflate deduction with reasoning.[5] Relations of deductive implication hold among propositions, or sets of them. Reasoning is psychological: it is a matter of what one believes and why. We cannot assume that, in reasoning to justified belief, one's premises entail that the belief is true. More charitably, there are contexts in which it makes sense to focus on what subjects take as evidence for their beliefs, as when we think of someone expressing an inference in words. When inference is in this way articulate, it may rely on or presuppose beliefs of the relevant kind. If I say to you, 'p, therefore q' it may follow that I believe if p then q, and that my inference is warranted only if I am antecedently justified in this belief. Here we focus on the grounds I am disposed to give. The mistake is to generalize from this. When a belief rests on evidence I do not or cannot articulate, I need not believe a conditional whose antecedent states my evidence in full.

Finally, and most importantly, the demand for antecedently justified belief is easily confused with a more plausible claim. In order to see this, we must distinguish 'propositional' from 'doxastic' justification. To be doxastically justified in believing p is to believe it with justification. Knowledge is the ideal case. Unlike knowledge, propositional justification does not require belief. It is, if you like, an entitlement to believe. The distinction is clearest when we have evidence for p. What one is propositionally justified in believing is what one's evidence supports, or makes epistemically probable, whether one believes it or not. To be doxastically justified by evidence is to believe p on the basis of that evidence, in the right sort of way. The idea that one is justified in believing p by evidence q only if one is antecedently justified in believing the conditional, if q then p, is ambiguous between a demand for

---

[5] Against this conflation, see, especially, Harman 1986: 3–6.

doxastic justification or justified belief and a demand for propositional justification:

In order to be justified in believing p by evidence q, one must have antecedent justification for the conditional, if q then p.

In my view, the most tempting source of the demand for antecedently justified belief is a failure to distinguish it from the principle just described. The former conflicts with Reductive Epistemology; but there is no good argument on its behalf. The latter may well be true; but there is no conflict.

We can see this if we consider, briefly, what supports the demand for antecedent justification, in propositional form. One argument is Bayesian: acquiring evidence q can increase the probability of p by conditionalization only if the prior probability of the relevant conditional is high.[6] A second argument draws on the principle of Reflection: if S knows that he would be justified in believing p by evidence q, he is already justified in believing the conditional, if q then p, loss of evidence aside. So long as we know in advance what our evidence would justify, we can use this principle to argue for the one above.[7] Neither argument is airtight. We can resist the first if we dispute the Bayesian machinery, the second by denying prior knowledge of epistemic facts.[8] Even if they work, these arguments leave the content of their conclusion somewhat dark. We know what it means to speak of propositional justification by evidence: it is what one's evidence supports, believe it or not. We can also make sense of non-evidentially justified belief, if only in negative terms.[9] The puzzle is what to make of groundless propositional justification, as when we apply the demand above to one's total evidence. A natural thought ties propositional justification to the capacity for doxastic justification

---

[6] Schiffer 2004; White 2006: §5.

[7] Here I adapt the argument from future justification in White 2006: §6.

[8] Weatherson 2007.

[9] See the treatment of intuitionist views in chapter one.

in idealized conditions. This prompts a final argument.[10] Suppose you are justified in believing p by evidence q. If you had the capacity to articulate your evidence in full, you would be justified in believing p on the basis of beliefs in which q is explicitly represented. Now consider a time before you acquire evidence q. If you had the further capacity for hypothetical reasoning, you could suppose q and conclude p on that assumption. If you grasp the relevant conditional, and nothing interferes with your beliefs about it, you could then use conditional proof, coming to believe if q then p. Thus, if you had enhanced capacities, you could form a justified belief in this conditional before you acquire evidence q. In general, however, if you could form a justified belief with enhanced capacities but no additional evidence, you are propositionally justified in believing its content on the evidence you have. It follows that you have propositional justification for the conditional, if q then p, antecedent to evidence q. This argument both motivates and clarifies the demand for antecedent justification.

Without endorsing it, we can see that this result coheres with Reductive Epistemology. When I know the worth of an act or agent, I do not typically know it by deduction from a conditional, if x is N then x is E, that is the object of non-evidentially justified belief. My knowledge rests on evidence that is not itself ethical, but which need not form the antecedent of a conditional I believe on other grounds. At the same time, that I do not believe a conditional of this kind is consistent with having the capacity to believe it, with non-evidential justification, in idealized conditions. If I could exploit my ethical judgement on the description of a case as well as I can when I occupy the case itself, if I could do so hypothetically and employ conditional proof, I could form a justified belief in the relevant conditional that does not rest on evidence at all. The problem is that I lack these capacities. In particular, my capacity for judgement on the

<hr />

[10] Inspired by Wedgwood, forthcoming; see also Cohen 2010.

evidence I possess outstrips my power to reason hypothetically from evidence described to me. This limits the scope for non-evidentially justified belief, as in Reductive Epistemology, but allows for propositional justification.

The upshot of these reflections is that it is not a condition of evidentially justified belief that one believe a conditional whose antecedent is one's evidence and whose consequent the content of one's belief. Still, it may follow from one's beliefs being justified by evidence, q, that one has propositional justification for this conditional, antecedent to q. It is then a consequence of Reductive Epistemology that we have non-evidential justification for ethical beliefs that we do not actually form.

This picture leaves the psychology of doxastic justification obscure. If not through conditional beliefs, how does evidence relate to what we know? We can begin with a platitude: evidentially justified belief is based on sufficient evidence: in some sense, one believes p because one has this evidence, though mere causation is not enough. Epistemologists dispute the nature of the 'basing relation'. Is it a matter of non-deviant causality? Is it a causal relation at all? Whatever it is, there is more to justified belief. Two people can believe the same thing on the basis of identical evidence, and yet one's belief be justified and the other's not. It matters not only where you start and where you end up, but how you get from one place to the other. Think about inference. There may be different ways to reason from p to q, some good, some not so good. You can reach the right conclusion, from a premise that in fact supports it, by defective reasoning. This need not involve a further premise; it is enough that one's pattern of inference is flawed. In that case, one's belief is based on sufficient evidence—this is not mere causation, but reasoning—without being doxastically justified.[11] The point can

[11] Harman argues on similar lines (Harman 1973: 30–1), though he builds the pattern of reasoning into the reason itself.

be generalized. If I am disposed to form beliefs in some irrational way, there will be room for epistemic luck. A belief may be derived, irrationally, from evidence of its truth. It is not thereby justified.

How to state the condition of justified belief that rules such accidents out? A natural thought is that, when S forms an evidentially justified belief, she manifests an epistemically reliable disposition: a disposition to form beliefs on the basis of evidence by which they are propositionally justified. In the special case of knowledge, she manifests a disposition that tracks the truth: it generates true beliefs when it issues in belief at all. In each case, there are questions about the scope of the relevant disposition— across what range of beliefs must one be reliable?—and about the threshold or ratio of reliability involved. Nothing will turn on these difficulties here; they belong to general epistemology. In relation to ethical knowledge, we can work with a simple formula: if you know that x is E, your knowledge manifests a reliable disposition, a disposition to believe the truth on adequate grounds.

In the context of Reductive Epistemology, the grounds in question are non-ethical and their relation to belief is not deductive. This picture has the striking consequence that ethical wisdom involves, and cannot be extricated from, the tendency to get non-ethical situations right. In a deductive model, we might think of ethical wisdom as the source of a conditional, if x is N then x is E, that we know without evidence; non-ethical knowledge provides the further premise, x is N; and logical competence does the rest. As I have argued, however, this model is not correct. Although we can separate one's evidence from what one makes of it, ethical judgement cannot be decomposed: we cannot filter off its purely ethical part. When I know you acted wrongly, believing that you hit a child, I must be sensitive to defeating conditions, situations in which it would have been permissible to do so. This sensitivity is at once ethical and empirical: it calls on the capacity to judge, of the circumstances that would make an ethical difference—the presence of a lethal insect on her arm, a dire threat, anaesthesia— which ones are likely to obtain. Reliability here depends on ordinary wisdom: a sense of how things go, non-ethically conceived, that only experience will teach.[12]

Even if it does not take a deductive form, ethical judgement need not be inarticulate. One may give reasons for one's verdict and rely on principles that guide and organize ethical thought. There are open questions here, about the nature of such principles, their defeasibility, and their role in reliable judgement. But there is no fundamental mystery. What the condition of reliability demands is nothing more than a disposition to form beliefs of one kind on the basis of others in a way that tracks, at least roughly, the conditionals involved in Ethical Supervenience. In a simple reliabilist epistemology, it would suffice for knowledge that one manifest this disposition in forming a true belief.[13] The possibility of knowledge in ethics would be safe.

Unfortunately, there are complications. Some turn on general doubts about reliabilism, as for instance its neglect of evidence in epistemic justification. That objection is unfair to the present view, since the disposition that issues in ethical knowledge is a disposition to believe the truth on adequate grounds. It draws on evidence of the sort described by Reductive Epistemology. More significant is the issue of epistemic luck, which is our central and defining theme. Of the sceptical arguments with which we began, one, the argument from ethical disagreement, has been addressed. We know how to resist the inference from fundamental disagreement to scepticism. The other arguments remain. Each can be cast as a challenge to the sufficiency of reliable belief. They ask, in different ways: what if our reliability is a matter of luck,

---

[12] On the role of 'worldly wisdom' in Aristotelian *phronesis*, see Hursthouse 2006.
[13] Russ Shafer-Landau holds something like this view, though he wrongly contrasts it with a model of inference or appeal to evidence (Shafer-Landau 2003: 270–4).

an accident or coincidence? Would that discovery conflict with our claim to knowledge or justified belief?

In the rest of this chapter, I confront a reading of these questions inspired by Hartry Field's critique of mathematical Platonism.[14] Field argues that, for the Platonist, our reliability about arithmetic would be a sheer coincidence, the chance correlation of fact and belief. It is thus incredible: mathematical Platonism leads to sceptical doubt. In section 2, Field's challenge is transposed to ethics and briefly compared with arguments by Sharon Street.[15] Against Field, I argue that doubts about coincidence must be qualified in a way that is fatal to their sceptical use. Against Street, I argue that it is licit to appeal to ethical knowledge as evidence of one's own reliability, as I do in response to Field. If this is right, the problem of coincidence can be solved.

2. COINCIDENCE

Field's argument begins by noting that our reliability about arithmetic involves a pervasive correlation of fact and belief. In general, if mathematicians believe an arithmetical proposition, the proposition is true. This correlation cries out for explanation. Why should these things go together, one a matter of psychology, the other of mathematics? Did it just happen to be so? According to Field, if our alleged reliability about arithmetic could not be explained, that fact would undermine our arithmetical beliefs. If we become aware of it, we should give them up. Field argues that, for the mathematical Platonist, this threat is real: since mathematical objects are mind-independent and causally inert, our reliability is inexplicable. If mathematical Platonism were true, there would be decisive grounds for mathematical scepticism.

---

[14] Field 1989: 25–30, 230–9.
[15] Street 2006, ms.

There is some question about the interpretation of this argument. As Field notes, the argument 'depends on the idea that we should view with suspicion any claim to know facts about a certain domain if we believe it impossible in principle to explain the reliability of our beliefs about that domain' (Field 1989: 233). But how exactly do we go from knowledge of inexplicability to scepticism? A striking feature of Field's approach is that, according to his intention, it 'does not depend on *any* theory of knowledge in the sense in which the causal theory is a theory of knowledge: that is, it does not depend on any assumption about the necessary and sufficient conditions for knowledge' (Field 1989: 232–3).[16] His argument is not that the fact of inexplicability conflicts with some condition of arithmetical knowledge, but that knowledge of inexplicability would take away our right to the relevant beliefs. Their justification is undermined.

In chapter three, we will consider a sceptical argument that does rely on explicability as a condition of knowledge. This argument may vindicate Field's suspicion; but it is not Field's argument. How, then, does his argument work? It rests on the view that an inexplicable correlation of fact and belief would be

altogether too much to swallow. It is rather as if someone claimed that his or her belief states about the daily happenings in a remote village in Nepal were nearly all ... true, despite the absence of any mechanism to explain the correlation between those belief states and the happenings in the village. Surely we should accept this only as a very last resort. (Field 1989: 26–7)

If we are looking for an argument that does not turn on a special connection between knowledge and explanation, what we are left with are doubts about coincidence. It is virtually axiomatic, one would think, that coincidences, or inexplicable correlations, are unlikely to occur. In general:

---

[16] Field here contrasts his argument with that of Paul Benacerraf (1973), though he acknowledges its influence.

COINCIDENCE: If I know that a correlation of facts would be inexplicable, I should doubt that the correlation obtains.

If arithmetical facts concern non-spatio-temporal objects independent of our beliefs, and if these facts are causally inert, as the Platonist contends, the correlation of mathematical fact and belief cannot be explained. By Coincidence, we should doubt that the correlation obtains. That is, we should doubt that our mathematical beliefs are generally true. Mathematical Platonism yields a sceptical result.[17]

Before relating this argument to ethics and assessing its force, some clarifications are worthwhile. First, being reliable is getting things mostly right. The sceptical conclusion is that one should doubt that one is reliable in this sense, a discovery that reverberates through one's beliefs, sapping their credibility. Second, explanations of reliability are permitted to appeal to the objects of the disputed beliefs. We could not explain the reliability of perception without relying on claims for which our warrant is itself perceptual. There is no harm in that. Accordingly, we are allowed to beg the question, assuming the truth of our beliefs, and asking whether, if they were true, our reliability could be explained. Finally, it is not enough to avoid Coincidence that we can explain why we are disposed to have the relevant beliefs and that the facts they represent are not in need of explanation. In an important discussion of Field, John Burgess and Gideon Rosen claim that 'there is in effect just one, sole, single, unique axiom [of set theory: that] the full cumulative hierarchy of sets exist' (Burgess and Rosen 1997: 45). Instead of a pervasive correlation between the items on two lists, we have a mere conjunction: that there is a full

---

[17] This formulation of Field's argument is close to that of Enoch 2010: §3.1; Schafer 2010: §3.3. Let me stress that, throughout this chapter, I am interested in questions of coincidence only so far as they relate to scepticism. I won't discuss the comparative claim that it counts in favour of alternatives to Platonism, or ethical realism, that they explain what Platonists and realists cannot. As chapter three suggests, I doubt that the claims of reliability 'explained' by constructivists are true.

cumulative hierarchy of sets and that we believe it. Since the existence of the hierarchy is necessary, we can reasonably reject the demand for an explanation of the first conjunct. And 'at least a very good beginning towards an explanation of [the second], of how and why standard set theory came to be believed, is given in standard histories' (Burgess and Rosen 1997: 45–6). As Burgess and Rosen concede, however, this fails to satisfy because it finds no connection between the conjuncts. In that respect, the truth of the conjunction remains a sheer coincidence. Suppose we meet at the DMV on Saturday morning. There is a reason why I am here, and a reason why you are, but if these reasons are unrelated, it is still a coincidence that we are here at the same time. In the relevant sense, the correlation is not explained.

The moral of these reflections is that Field's challenge is neither trivial nor impossible to meet. In some cases, we can do so, as for instance when we give a causal account of perception, or when some domain of facts is 'response-dependent' or constituted by our beliefs. In others, the task looks much more difficult: what can the mathematical Platonist say?

A similar question can be posed in ethics. If ethical facts are independent of the attitudes we would have upon reflection, as so-called 'ethical realists' claim, what could explain the reliability of our ethical beliefs?[18] If the answer is that nothing could, Coincidence applies, to sceptical effect. In a different context, we would need to be more precise about the content of ethical realism and the sorts of explanations it allows. That will happen in chapter three; it is not urgent here. Instead, I will argue that Coincidence is false. Before that, I pause to compare the problem of coincidence with an 'evolutionary critique' of ethical realism.

According to the evolutionary critique, the most basic dispositions that govern ethical thought can be explained by natural

---

[18] This definition of realism is due to Street 2006: 110–11.

selection, in terms that do not advert to ethical facts.[19] The purported implication is well expressed by Sharon Street:

Of course it's *possible* that as a matter of sheer chance, some large portion of our evaluative judgements ended up true, due to a happy coincidence between the realist's independent evaluative truths and the evaluative direction in which natural selection tended to push us, but this would require a fluke of luck that's not only extremely unlikely, in view of the huge universe of logically possible evaluative judgements and truths, but also astoundingly convenient to the realist. (Street 2006: 122)

On a natural reading, the argumentative strategy here is Field's. The background premise is Coincidence, and the relevance of evolution is simply as a place for realists to turn in trying to explain the reliability of ethical beliefs. We may question whether it is the only place,[20] but if it is, the shape of the argument is clear.

Another reading is possible, however. Street spends considerable time establishing the role of natural selection in the evolution of ethics (Street 2006: §4). She calls this the 'first premise' of her argument, and worries that the influence of evolution is, by the realist's lights, 'distorting' and 'illegitimate' (Street 2006: 121–2). If her argument goes by Coincidence, this emphasis is misleading. It is the realist who needs to explain our reliability, and the crucial claim is that she cannot do this, regardless of what in fact explains our ethical beliefs. The problem of coincidence would be no less severe if our basic dispositions of ethical thought could not be explained in evolutionary terms. Street's framing thus suggests a different argument, one that proceeds not by way of Coincidence, but from the idea of 'genetic undermining': that some accounts of the origin of a belief show it to be doxastically unjustified. It is in this spirit that Richard Joyce imagines a pill that makes one form beliefs about Napoleon, independent of their truth:

---

[19] Street 2006: 125–30; Joyce 2006: Ch. 6.
[20] Compare Street 2006: 134–5, 155.

Suppose . . . that you discover beyond any doubt that you were slipped one of these pills a few years ago. Does this undermine all the beliefs you have concerning Napoleon? Of course it does. . . . This wouldn't show the belief to be *false*, but until you find some reliable evidence to confirm or disconfirm your Napoleon beliefs, you should take the antidote. . . . The intention of this make-believe scenario is to prime us for an analogous epistemological conclusion regarding an evolved moral sense. (Joyce 2006: 181)

There is no doubt that certain explanations of belief (or knowledge of those explanations) do preclude doxastic justification. In a genetic undermining argument, the appeal to evolution by natural selection is meant to be an explanation of this kind.[21] The challenge for the evolutionary sceptic is to find a condition of justification that applies not only to empirical but ethical belief, and that requires the kind of explanation ethical realists cannot give. We will come back to this requirement in chapter three. Here the point is to contrast genetic undermining with the appeal to Coincidence in Field and Street. In the rest of this section, I focus on the latter, urging two conclusions: that Coincidence must be qualified; and that, once it is qualified, it lacks force against even the most uncompromising ethical realist.

According to Coincidence, we should be sceptical of unexplained and inexplicable correlations. On occasion, we have positive evidence that a correlation does not obtain, or is improbable. In light of its generality, however, such evidence is not the basis of Coincidence. Assuming ethical realism, what evidence do we have *against* a correlation of ethical fact and belief?[22] Instead, Coincidence rests on a priori doubt: a rational prejudice against the inexplicable. As a principle of indifference assigns equal prior probability to outcomes that our evidence does not discriminate, and therefore low probability to each when the possible outcomes

---

[21] For this interpretation, see Joyce 2006: Ch. 6; Kahane 2011. An important precursor is Stroud 1981.
[22] This point is emphasized in Schafer 2010: §2.

are many, so, we might suppose, the prior probability of an inexplicable coincidence is low. It is this thought that underlies the rhetoric of Coincidence, the view that our reliability would be incredible if it could not be explained, that there would be a miraculous correlation between independent matters of fact. What convenient luck! If our reliability is inexplicable, we should lose confidence in it, and thus in our ethical beliefs.

Even if we grant this prejudice, however, the sceptical inference is too quick. For a priori doubts about coincidence, if warranted, are defeasible. In the most mundane example, I am justified in doubting that we will both be at the DMV on Saturday morning, given that our choices are independent. Nothing would explain our meeting there. Still, if I decide to go to the DMV, and I see you with my own eyes, it would be madness to doubt the admittedly inexplicable conjunction of facts. When I consider a more extraordinary conjunction, my scepticism should be greater. How likely is it that everyone in my Department would be at the DMV at the same time? Yet as I look around, there they are! Here I might justifiably cast about for an explanation, something to connect our paths. But if I do not succeed, so be it. My knowledge is not undermined.

Examples like these have some impurity, since I have empirical evidence about the likelihood of various DMV encounters: my doubts are not wholly a priori. But the point survives translation into cases more abstract and less agreeable. Think of inexplicable correlations in the colours of marbles drawn from bags, about which I have no antecedent evidence. The most we can plausibly say is that the prior probability of an inexplicable coincidence is low, and that I should not believe in one *unless I am otherwise justified in doing so*, as when I have sufficient evidence of each coincident fact, regardless of their connection. Coincidence must therefore be revised:

COINCIDENCE QUALIFIED: If I know that a correlation of facts would be inexplicable, *and I am not otherwise justified in accepting it*, I should doubt that the correlation obtains.

The qualification is momentous. In order to extract a sceptical verdict from the inexplicability of reliable belief by way of Coincidence Qualified, one would need to show that we are not otherwise justified in believing ourselves reliable—that we are not justified in accepting our reliability in a way that is independent of how it is explained. Let the ethical realist concede that there is no explanation of reliability, any more than there is for the concurrent presence of my colleagues at the DMV or the series of blue marbles drawn from the bag. So long as she insists that I am independently justified in my ethical beliefs, and in believing that I have them, she can exploit the clause that separates Coincidence Qualified from Coincidence. We may rightly cast about for an explanation of reliable belief, but if we do not succeed, so be it. Our knowledge is not undermined. In the absence of a sceptical argument against the justification of ethical beliefs on non-explanatory grounds—an argument that would make Field's challenge redundant—there is nothing to be said.

It might be argued, against this deflationary view, that correlations may be so pervasive and so striking that if they turned out inexplicable, we should doubt the evidence on their behalf. Think of Hume's argument against miracles, according to which their vanishing probability counts against the testimony of those who claim to have witnessed them (Hume 1748: §10). Whatever the force of this argument in its original setting, however, it is not effective here. First, the minimal probability Hume cites depends on accumulated evidence of the laws of nature, 'and as a firm and unalterable experience has established these laws, the proof against a miracle, from the very nature of the fact, is as entire as any argument from experience can possibly be imagined' (Hume 1748: §10, para. 12). Not so in the present case, which relies on a priori doubts about coincidence whose force is significantly weaker.

Second, the extent of the miracle involved in ethical knowledge, even for the realist, is far from clear.[23] If her model is one of deduction from principles known without evidence, the realist may insist on the correlation of a single principle and belief: just you and me at the DMV. Or the principles may be several, but few.

Finally, however great the coincidence of reliable belief, its epistemic upshot is unclear. Whether I should doubt a correlation that cannot be explained, all things considered, turns not only on its extent but on the strength of evidence on which my belief in the correlation rests. Hume makes the corresponding point when he allows that a miracle *might* be established by sufficient testimony, against our 'firm and unalterable experience': 'suppose, all authors, in all languages, agree, that, from the first of January 1600, there was total darkness over the whole world for eight days: . . . It is evident, that our present philosophers, instead of doubting the fact, ought to receive it as certain' (Hume 1748: §10, para. 36). His claim is that, as a matter of fact, we have inadequate evidence for any religious miracle, weighed against our enormous evidence for the laws of nature—not that this would be impossible. Hume's contrast can be generalized. When I look around the DMV and catch a distant glimpse of seemingly familiar faces, my evidence is weak. In light of the extraordinary coincidence involved, I should doubt that the whole Department is there. As my evidence improves, however, with a second glance or an exchange of quizzical smiles, my doubts should fade. Here they are, on Saturday morning at the DMV, by pure luck. The same thing goes for a priori doubts about coincidence of arbitrarily high degree. Such doubts do not have sceptical import, on balance, if the justification that compensates for them is correspondingly strong. The ethical

---

[23] For responses in much this spirit, see Enoch 2010: §5.3; Schafer 2010: §3.3. See also Burgess and Rosen 1997: 45–6, cited in the text above.

realist should claim to have justification for her ethical beliefs, and for the belief that she has them, sufficient to outweigh the prior probability of her being reliable, however low. In order to be effective, a sceptical appeal to Coincidence Qualified must refute this claim. It needs an independent proof of a sceptical conclusion: that even when they are justified, the epistemic standing of ethical beliefs is not sufficiently strong.[24]

The last point seems to me the deepest. Since they are defeasible, a priori doubts about coincidence cannot undermine our beliefs all by themselves. They must be weighed against the justification of those beliefs. A case must be made against the strength of evidence available in a Reductive Epistemology, or of non-evidential justification in a deductive intuitionist view. We have seen no hint of this.

One issue remains. According to the story I have been telling on behalf of the ethical realist, Coincidence is false and the challenge of its qualified version can be met. I am entitled to accept the correlation of ethical fact and belief involved in reliability if, and because, the justification of my beliefs, and of their self-ascription, is sufficiently strong. That I have true beliefs is evidence, by deductive or explanatory inference, of my reliability. This reasoning can seem bizarre, or worse. In using my beliefs to establish my own reliability, don't I illicitly beg the question? An argument for reliability from ethical premises, together with

[24] At one point, Field seems to concede this demand (Field 1989: 238–9). He frames his conclusion as one of epistemic conflict: inexplicable reliability versus reasons for belief. But he calls this 'a case of competing arguments' and holds that 'for a satisfactory view to be achieved, we must find a way of disarming one of [them]' (Field 1989: 239). We must show that there are no reasons for mathematical belief, conceived in Platonist terms, or that there is nothing wrong with inexplicable reliability. To take the first path is to give the independent proof for which I am pressing. What I deny is that the Platonist must take the second. She can admit that there are grounds for doubt about reliability, given that it is inexplicable, while insisting that such doubts can be outweighed. We need not show them to be unfounded or inauthentic, that there is nothing wrong with inexplicable reliability, only that their force is limited. They do not defeat the justification of our beliefs.

the claim that I believe them, looks suspiciously circular, an attempt to pull myself up by my epistemic bootstraps. If the belief that I am reliable cannot be justified in this way, the sceptical argument is restored. All it needs is Coincidence Qualified: if I know that a correlation of facts would be inexplicable, and I am not otherwise justified in accepting it, I should doubt that the correlation obtains. In the concluding section of this chapter, I argue that belief in reliability *can* be justified on ethical and introspective grounds.

3. BEGGING THE QUESTION

In a perceptive discussion of these topics, Sharon Street notes the defeasibility of Coincidence, or something like it, but persists in her critique (Street ms.: §8). She gives an example in which I learn that I have won the New York State Lottery. Although I know that winning the lottery is a matter of inexplicable luck, this fact is not enough to undermine the belief that I have won. It is not always wrong to believe that a coincidence has occurred. Street claims, however, that the sceptical problem survives. As she insists, the lottery case is one in which I have independent evidence of having won: 'I got some sort of official phone call, the press showed up, and the checks started rolling in.' It remains true that, 'if the odds of your having won the lottery are very low, and you have no non-trivially-question-begging reason to think that you did, then you should conclude that you probably didn't' (Street ms.: §9). Street holds that, in general, if one believes in a correlation one knows to be inexplicable, one needs evidence of its occurrence that does not simply beg the question. This is what the ethical realist lacks.

In saying this, Street does not deny that we can give non-question-begging arguments for particular ethical claims, as when we derive them from others. The problem is not about individual judgements. What the realist cannot do, according to

Street, is to give reasons that support the total system of ethical beliefs that she accepts against consistent alternatives. If the realist continues to believe that her convictions correlate with the facts, while competing convictions do not, she 'is in no better position than the person who question-beggingly insists that she won the New York State Lottery, even though she has no reason to think so apart from the fact that she entered it' (Street ms.: §9).

The charge is initially puzzling. If the realist adopts a Reductive Epistemology, she will contrast the ethical case with Street's lottery by citing non-ethical evidence. If this evidence supports her beliefs, she is not in the position of having no reason to think they are true apart from the fact that she has them. The non-evidential intuitionist will draw a different contrast, holding her beliefs to be justified without evidence. Even if she can give no further reason for them, her position is quite different from that of the lottery optimist, whose belief that she won has no support. A response of this kind is available only if our beliefs in fact possess the relevant virtues. But that is fine. The sceptical argument needs to show that, if ethical realism is true, no one is entitled to ethical beliefs, not just that some beliefs cannot be justified. If we have non-evidential or non-ethical support for our beliefs, our epistemic position is quite different from that of someone who claims to have won the lottery simply because she has a ticket. Finally, it does not matter to this contrast that the lottery optimist might *claim* non-evidential right to her belief, or cite some arbitrary evidence. It is not the belief that one is justified that counts, but the fact of it.[25]

On a more charitable reading, Street does not merely assert the absence of justification for ethical beliefs that could overcome a priori doubts or distinguish such beliefs from the lottery hypothesis. She argues that the sources of support available to

---

[25] For a similar point against astrology, see Williamson 2007: 241; this section is more generally indebted to his discussion.

the realist—like those described in the previous paragraph—illicitly beg the question. This was the issue left open at the end of section 2.

In order to assess the problem, we need a sharper account of what is involved in begging the question, and what is supposed to be wrong with it. Notoriously, all valid arguments 'beg the question' in the sense that one cannot consistently accept their premises unless one accepts the relevant conclusion. That is not an epistemic defect! A more tempting definition ties begging the question to dialectical efficacy.[26] One's justification is non-question-begging, in this sense, just in case it could rationally persuade someone who is sceptical of one's claims. A case can be made that the justifications available to Reductive Epistemology and non-evidential intuitionism fail this test. Take the latter conception first. If ethical beliefs are non-evidentially justified, and the belief that I am reliable rests on ethical claims together with the fact that I believe them, what can I say to someone who doubts that my beliefs are true? So long as he knows what my beliefs are, he denies the ethical premises of my argument, premises for which I have no further grounds. The justification for thinking that I am reliable begs the question against this figure: there is nothing in it that could rationally persuade him. Something similar holds in a Reductive Epistemology. Here ethical beliefs are justified by non-ethical evidence. On the basis of their contents, and the fact that I believe them, I am justified in thinking that my beliefs are true, from which I infer my own reliability. Although the evidence on which I draw is not itself ethical, someone who doubts my reliability in ethics will doubt the relevance of this evidence—assuming he knows what I believe and why. Once he makes that move, there are no grounds that I can cite on behalf of my beliefs, or of the claim that I am reliable, that could rationally persuade him that I am right.

[26] As in Pryor 2004: 369.

What is less clear is that there is anything wrong with the predicament in which I find myself, on either view. For it cannot be a condition of justification in general that it be dialectically effective against the sceptic. That premise would fuel a more pervasive scepticism.[27] Confronted with someone who doubts the reliability of perception, there are no grounds that I could give for my perceptual beliefs, or their reliability, that could rationally persuade him. Given his doubts, it would be irrational to accept my evidence. It does not follow that my beliefs are unjustified. Nor have we seen an argument that this is true when reliability cannot be explained: that the inexplicability of reliable belief creates a demand for dialectically effective grounds. Why should the standard of evidence change when a particular kind of evidence, the kind that would support explanatory inference, cannot be found? Coincidence Qualified is qualified enough. It asks for justification sufficient to outweigh the a priori prejudice against the inexplicable. This is a condition on strength of justification, not dialectical role.

There is another way to interpret claims about begging the question, not in terms of dialectical efficacy but of 'epistemic bootstrapping'. As I will argue, this interpretation gives a more plausible explanation of disquiet about the justifications of reliability offered so far. It will turn out, however, that such disquiet is misplaced.

A good way to begin is with an argument for the reliability of perception that seems profoundly flawed. This argument turns on perceptual claims that are justified by how things seem. Suppose I am presented with a series of colour cards. The first card looks red, so I conclude that it is. I go on to self-ascribe the experience involved, inferring that the card both looks and is red. From this I deduce, trivially, that on this occasion, things

[27] See Pryor 2004: 370; also Williamson 2007: 238–41 on the 'dialectical standard of evidence'.

looked the way they were. I then repeat the procedure. The next card looks green. Self-ascribing the experience and forming the belief it warrants, I infer that, once again, things looked the way they were. Again, I repeat the procedure. Eventually I conclude, with satisfaction, that I have reliable colour vision!

If this reasoning seems absurd, it is disturbingly similar to reasoning in which one infers the reliability of one's ethical beliefs from the contents of those beliefs and the fact that one has them. But that is just what I advised the ethical realist to do. It is easy to suspect that something has gone wrong.

Now, some resist this verdict, even in the perceptual case, holding that the failure of the repetitive argument is merely dialectical.[28] Though it is useless against the sceptic, we can learn that our perceptions are reliable by arguing in this way. In order to make things difficult for the realist, I will assume that the argument is more seriously flawed. It is illicit to conclude, on the basis of how things look, that appearances do not deceive: that if the card looks red, it is. There is a standard picture of the defect in this reasoning.[29] According to this account, I am justified in thinking that the first card is red, since that is how it looks, and I am justified in thinking that it looks that way. What is more, I am justified in believing that the card both looks and is red, that this is not a case of non-veridical experience. (There may be cases in which one is justified in believing p and justified in believing q without being justified in believing p and q, as when one's degree of justification is marginal or weak. But this is not one of them.) The problem is that I cannot in this way *acquire* propositional justification for the conditional, if the card looks red, it is. The only evidence I have gained is that the card looks red, which is not evidence that appearances do not deceive. If I am justified in thinking that things look the way they are, my justification does

---

[28] Pryor 2004.
[29] Shared by White 2006: §7; Cohen 2010.

not come from the fact of how they look. We can reach the same conclusion in a different way, through a principle considered in section 1:

In order to be justified in believing p by evidence q, one must have antecedent justification for the conditional, if q then p.

In order to be justified in believing that the card is red on the basis of visual evidence, as in the argument above, I must have antecedent justification for the conditional, if the card looks red, it is. I cannot acquire this justification from the fact that it looks red.

The application to ethics is apparently straightforward. If the reliability of my beliefs is inexplicable, the only evidence I have that they are reliable is evidence that appeals to their truth. That my beliefs are true is something I deduce in turn from the contents of those beliefs—which I take to be ethical facts—and the fact that I believe them. If this is not a way to justify the claim of true belief, because it begs the question in the manner we have just explained, the argument for reliability stalls. I need antecedent justification to believe that, in ethics, what I believe is true. Since I lack such justification, the problem of coincidence returns.

This is, I think, the most seductive version of Street's complaint, that ethical realists beg the question when they argue for the reliability of ethical belief. The comparison on which it rests is, however, skewed. The arguments for reliable belief in Reductive Epistemology and non-evidential intuitionism differ crucially from the argument about perception. The basic contrast is this. When I argue by perceptual bootstrapping, I attempt to show that appearances do not deceive using evidence that consists, ultimately, in appearance itself. It is as if I am using a stick to measure its own length: I am using evidence to confirm its own veridicality. The ethical case is different. Although I attempt to justify the claim of true belief by way of the belief at hand, I do not use that belief as evidence of its truth. My belief is not the ultimate source of justification: it is justified by non-ethical evidence, or by non-evidential right. Instead of testing evidence against itself, I confirm the accuracy of belief by appeal to justification for its truth.

We can the put the point in terms that echo those above. In the perceptual case, the problem is that my evidence, that the card looks red, does not in fact support my conclusion, that appearances do not deceive. That the card looks red may be evidence that it is red; it is not evidence for the conditional, if the card looks red, it is. By contrast, in Reductive Epistemology, my evidence is distinct from the item whose accuracy is being assessed. What I have is evidence that x is N, where necessarily, if x is N then x is E. Since it counts as evidence that x is E, my evidence supports the conditional, if I believe that x is E, my belief is true. In structure, at least, this is no different from any other case of evidentially grounded belief. If I have evidence that it will rain tomorrow, and so conclude that it will, introspective knowledge of the belief that it will rain warrants the further claim that one of my beliefs is true. There is nothing untoward in this. The same thing holds for non-evidential views: if I am entitled to believe that x is E, not on the basis of evidence, I am entitled to believe that, if I believe that x is E, I have a true belief.

It is easy to see how this contrast could be missed. For it is true that, in arguing for the reliability of ethical belief, one must rely on ethical beliefs, as one relies on perceptual appearances in epistemic bootstrapping. The difference is that, with perception, the appearances make up one's evidence; in the ethical case, one's beliefs, and their contents, do not. They are intermediate steps in an argument for reliability, not its ultimate ground. The source of propositional justification in this argument is non-ethical or non-evidential; it is not one's beliefs themselves. While perceptual appearances cannot directly show that appearances do not deceive, the justification of ethical belief can show that one's beliefs are true.

Where it is not simply confused, the temptation to deny this contrast marks the persistence of the Empirical Model and the

Pure Coherence View. These theories treat the justification of ethical belief as a function of ethical attitudes: intuitions as appearances or judgements. If one mistakes the methodological truism, that we must work from what we believe, for an epistemology of Pure Coherence or reflective equilibrium, one will be unable to see the difference between perceptual bootstrapping and the argument for reliability in ethics that goes through ethical belief.[30] In each case, one seems to endorse the reliability of one's evidence on the basis of that evidence itself. As we have seen, however, both the Empirical Model and the Pure Coherence View are false. One's ethical beliefs are not the source of evidence in ethics. In arguing for reliability by way of those beliefs, one draws on a further mode of justification, non-evidential or non-ethical. One pulls oneself up with the help of this support, not by one's epistemic bootstraps.

The conclusion for which I am pressing is this: once we reject epistemologies of intuition and coherence, as we did in chapter one, there is nothing illicit or question-begging in the justification of reliability by way of ethical beliefs. If those beliefs are non-evidentially justified or supported by non-ethical evidence, and if their warrant is sufficiently strong, it can outweigh the a priori doubts about coincidence on which Field and Street rely. A sceptical argument from coincidence must cast doubt not only on the prospects for an explanation of reliability, in a realist view, but on the strength of support our ethical beliefs enjoy. It needs a sceptical premise that the realist need not and should not concede.

It does not follow from this that inexplicability is epistemically irrelevant, only that its relevance does not derive from the general epistemology of coincidence. Field's strategy, and the sceptical doubts inspired by it, are misconceived. This leaves a final argument for ethical scepticism. Its focus is not coincidence, as such,

---

[30] Does it follow that Street's argument is sound on the assumption of Pure Coherence? Not exactly. What follows is that we cannot respond to it as I have done. If the claim of reliability is justified in a Pure Coherence View, despite being inexplicable, it is justified not through ethical beliefs, but by non-evidential right.

but the conception of knowledge as non-accidentally true belief. Accidental truth matters to epistemology not because inexplicable correlations are rare, but because it conflicts with the claim to know. In the following chapter, I explore the nature of knowledge as a special case of justified belief, arguing that no-accident conditions place constraints on what can be known. If there is ethical knowledge, our attitudes must be constitutively bound up with the facts. The threat of such a view is that we will be forced into relativism—if the facts depend on what we think, and our convictions vary—or to implausible predictions of convergence in belief. In principle, I claim, we can avoid both risks. Whether we can do so in practice is a question left till the very end.

3

Knowledge

At a certain point in chapter two, I distinguished the problem of coincidence, which was its principal topic, from another form of evolutionary critique. Both arguments assume that the evolutionary explanation of ethical belief does not appeal to, or depend upon, ethical facts. According to the problem of coincidence, the challenge is then to explain our reliability in some other way. Those who press the problem doubt that it can be done. The argument from genetic undermining is, by contrast, more direct. It contends that, since the explanation of ethical beliefs by evolution is wholly independent of ethical facts, those beliefs are epistemically undermined. This genetic discovery kills whatever claim to justification they would otherwise have.

The genetic undermining argument is the application to ethical belief and evolutionary explanation of a general claim about epistemic defeat. There are different versions of this claim, and different ways to motivate it, but a representative source is Barry Stroud in 'Evolution and the Necessities of Thought':[1]

[Some] explanations of the origin or retention of a belief are such that once we accept them we can no longer hold the belief in question or see it as defensible. Someone who hallucinates a bed covered with leaves and on that basis believes that the bed before him is covered with leaves does not thereby know that the bed is covered with leaves, even if it is.

---

[1] For a related argument, cited by Joyce 2006: Ch. 6, see Harman 1977: Ch. 1.

Someone who dreams, and thereby comes to believe, that Goldbach's conjecture is necessarily true does not on that basis know that it is necessarily true, even if it is.... [Even] if the truth of such explanations does not logically imply the falsity of what is believed, a person accepting such explanations as an account of his own beliefs is no longer entitled to ... hold those beliefs.... A belief that is shown to be solely the result of a hallucination or a dream is thereby discredited because the truth or probable truth of what is believed plays no role in the explanation of the fact that it is believed. (Stroud 1981: 55–6)

Although we can be gripped by it, there is something odd about this line of thought. We sometimes have evidence against the correlation of fact and belief: that beliefs caused in some particular way are unlikely to be true, and that the evidence for those beliefs is unreliable. When we discover that a belief was caused in this way, its support is undermined. But that is not our position in ethics. We do not know in advance that beliefs explained by evolution are probably false. That is a claim we are trying to assess.

Suppose we grant, for the sake of argument, that there is an explanation of ethical beliefs, in evolutionary terms, that does not cite ethical facts nor any facts explained by them. We can add, if this is something more, that ethical facts are irrelevant to the *best* explanation of our beliefs. Why should this make epistemic trouble for those beliefs, unless they were supported by explanatory inference? Let us admit that there is no way to justify ethical beliefs by inference to their own best explanation. One source of possible support has been removed. But as we saw in chapter one, the refuted conception of evidence in ethics is independently implausible. If ethical beliefs are justified, they are justified in other ways.

In *The Evolution of Morality*, Richard Joyce effectively concedes this point.[2] Having argued that moral facts are redundant in the

<hr>

[2] The concession is a bit unclear, since earlier sections make unqualified claims of epistemic undermining: 'our moral beliefs are products of a process that is entirely independent of their truth, which forces the recognition that we have no grounds one way or the other for maintaining these beliefs' (Joyce 2006: 211; see also

explanation of moral beliefs, he asks whether 'moral beliefs can be shown to be justified irrespective of the ontological status of the facts that make them true' (Joyce 2006: 211). He claims that they cannot—but his arguments are ones we have already discussed. Thus, he cites Sinnott-Armstrong (2002) on the need for inferential justification in the face of disagreement, objecting to intuitionist views. As we saw in chapter one, this argument illicitly runs together non-inferential justification, as in perception, with justification that does not rest on evidence at all. The former may be threatened by disagreement; the latter is not, at least not so much. What is more, Joyce ignores the prospect of a Reductive Epistemology, on which the evidence for ethical beliefs consists in evidence for the facts in virtue of which an ethical proposition is, or would be, true. If this conception of evidence fails, what is the argument against it? Not anything we have seen so far.

Our version of Reductive Epistemology is, admittedly, incomplete. It specifies the evidence for ethical propositions. But there is more to justified belief. In chapter two, I gave a condition of reliability for evidential justification: if one's belief is justified by evidence, one manifests an epistemically reliable disposition, a disposition to form beliefs on the basis of evidence by which they are propositionally justified. In the special case of knowledge, one manifests a disposition that tracks the truth: it tends to generate only true beliefs. The advocate of genetic undermining might propose a supplement, inspired by Stroud: one is doxastically justified in believing p only if the truth or probable truth of p plays a role in explaining one's belief. Since the truth or probable truth of ethical propositions is irrelevant to the explanation of ethical beliefs, such beliefs are never justified. Some will dispute the explanatory claim, which we have been willing to grant. More relevant here are doubts about the required epistemology. How

§§6.1–6.2). On balance, I take Joyce to qualify this view, which is restricted to explanatory or (what he calls) 'metaphysical' vindications of moral belief.

does the new proposal leave room for justified beliefs about the future? Their truth does not explain why they are held. Are these beliefs explained by their 'probable truth'? What does that involve? Even if this problem can be solved, why should the target of the argument, the ethical anti-sceptic, admit that the premise is true? In this context, it is utterly tendentious to assume, as a condition of justified belief, that the facts believed play a suitable explanatory role.[3]

That will not be assumed in the arguments to come. At the same time, it is difficult to accept that there is no connection at all between the facts in ethics and what we believe them to be, that the relationship is one of absolute independence. What was wrong with the problem of coincidence was not discomfort with this idea—that the correlation between fact and belief in ethics is wholly inexplicable—but the way in which it was motivated. We should be disturbed, not by the prospect of inexplicable correlation, as such, but of inexplicably true belief. This prospect is a threat to ethical knowledge. One cannot know that p if it is an accident that one's belief is true. But if the facts in ethics are independent of what we think, how could it fail to be an accident when we believe the truth?

This chapter develops and extends the problem of ethical knowledge. It defends an explanatory conception of non-accidental truth, applies this conception to ethics, and asks how its conditions could be met. Its verdict is that ethical knowledge is possible only if the facts in ethics are constitutively bound to our beliefs. The challenge is to reconcile this claim with the objectivity of ethical facts and with the limits of convergence in belief. As we will see in chapter four, this challenge can be met by appeal to human nature, and to ethical theories inspired by David Hume. We will ask what

[3] Compare what is now the standard response to Benacerraf 1973. Benacerraf appeals to a causal theory of knowledge in an argument against mathematical Platonism. But the Platonist will reject the causal theory.

such theories mean for justification as well as knowledge, and whether any of them could be true.

1. NO ACCIDENT

When S knows that p, it is no accident that her belief is true. Versions of this idea have been commonplace in epistemology since Gettier (1963). His examples of justified true belief that do not count as knowledge are ones in which it is a matter of luck or accident that someone believes the truth. The most ambitious thought inspired by Gettier is that knowledge just *is* non-accidentally true belief. Thus Peter Unger once proposed, as necessary and sufficient for factual knowledge, 'a complete absence of the accidental' in the relation of fact and belief (Unger 1968: 159). Although it may be an accident that p, and an accident that S was in a position to know that p, it must be 'not at all accidental' that S is right about whether p. In developing his view, Unger takes the concept of an accident as primitive. The views we will be considering differ from Unger's in two main ways. First, they purport to give necessary not sufficient conditions for knowing that p. There may be requirements that go beyond non-accidental truth, as it is articulated here. Second, they attempt to spell out what is involved in its being 'no accident' that one's belief is true.

According to a recently influential view, an accident is an event that fails to occur in some nearby possible world,[4] and the no-accident condition is one of epistemic 'safety': when S knows that p, most nearby worlds in which S believes that p are ones in which p is true.[5] In the relevant sense, a 'nearby' world is one that could easily have been the case. Despite its appeal, I resist the

---

[4] See Pritchard 2005: 130–1.
[5] Sainsbury 1997; Sosa 1999, 2005.

safety interpretation of non-accidental truth. As I argue, we should think of epistemic accidents not in modal but explanatory terms. In making this shift, which is motivated by general reflections on accidental truth, we extend the scope of the no-accident condition and expose the problem of ethical knowledge.

Begin with cases that make trouble for safety, as when I am threatened by counterfactual deception.[6] Suppose you have planned an illusion in which it will look to me that I am wearing my watch while you have secretly swiped it away. You are prevented at the final moment, by some bizarre bad luck. Since your plan has failed, and I have no reason to suspect it, I know that I am wearing my watch on the basis of veridical perception. Still, there are nearby possible worlds in which I am wrong. My belief is unsafe, but it counts as knowledge.

In counterfactual deception, the safety condition appears to be too strong. Elsewhere it seems too weak. Thus safety is vacuously satisfied for knowledge of necessary truths. When it is necessary that p, there are no nearby possible worlds in which I falsely believe that p. Yet it is surely possible to believe the truth by accident, or through epistemic luck, even in logic or mathematics.

In *Knowledge and its Limits*, Williamson briefly considers an example of this kind:

Let p be a mathematical truth, and therefore a necessary truth. Thus no case in which one falsely believes p is possible; yet one can still doubt p by doubting the reliability of the methods which led one to believe p. After all, someone with great faith in a certain coin might decide to believe p if it comes up heads and to believe $\sim p$ if it comes up tails; if he believes p because the coin came up heads, he does not know p, although he could not have believed p falsely. His belief fails to count as knowledge because the method by which he reached it could just as easily have led to a false belief in a different proposition. (Williamson 2000: 181–2)

---

[6] A possibility explored in Neta and Rohrbaugh 2004.

On Williamson's proposal, when S knows that p, she knows it on the basis of a method, m, whose output could not easily have been false: most nearby worlds in which S forms a belief by m are ones in which that belief is true.[7] This explains why Williamson's case is not a case of knowledge. It might also help with counterfactual deception. Although my belief that p is unsafe, given your planned illusion, the method by which I formed that belief can meet Williamson's condition. If method m is relying on veridical perception, nearby worlds in which I form a belief by my actual method are ones in which the belief is true.

Questions could be raised, here, about the identity of methods. Am I disposed to form beliefs on the basis of veridical perception? Or of perceptual appearance, as such? But whatever we make of this, the weakness of the view remains. We can describe a variation of the coin case in which I am disposed to believe p if the coin comes up heads and to remain agnostic otherwise.[8] Given that p is a necessary truth, this method could not easily lead me astray. Yet without an account of why I am using this method—if my method is entirely arbitrary—it is not a source of knowledge that p. The belief it generates is accidentally true.

If safety of methods is not enough to exclude such accidents, we might turn to 'adherence' instead. Adherence is the converse of safety on which, when S knows that p, most nearby worlds in which p is true are ones in which S believes it.[9] In the modified coin case, there are nearby worlds in which I fail to believe p because the coin comes up tails, even though p, being necessary, is true. But this does little to help. First, there is no general requirement of adherence for knowledge. I can know the truth by a method whose threshold for delivering a verdict is extremely

---

[7] Related suggestions appear in Sosa 1999: 149, and Sosa 2005.

[8] Yamada 2011: 88.

[9] The concept of adherence is due to Robert Nozick, who applies it to knowledge of necessary truths (Nozick 1981: 186–7).

high, so high that it virtually always leaves me agnostic. A method of this kind may be epistemically poor in other respects; but it can be a source of knowledge.[10] Second, there are cases of accidentally true belief in which the condition of adherence is met. Consider, for instance, innate beliefs. If I am hard-wired to believe p as soon as I am able to comprehend it, and p is necessarily true, I am using a method that could not easily fail to yield true belief. Still, if the innateness of the belief is unrelated to its truth, it is an accident that my belief that p is true. The same point can be made for reliable methods that I am induced to use in irrelevant but not capricious ways.[11] Suppose you aim to implant in me, mechanically—not through persuasion or evidence—the disposition to believe p as soon as I am able to comprehend it. You have no idea whether this disposition is reliable; you simply want me to have it. If you are sufficiently powerful, you may succeed. If p is a necessary truth, my disposition to believe p will satisfy both safety and adherence even though it is an accident that my belief is true. Cases of the same kind hold for contingent facts. Thus, supposing Kripke (1980) is right about the essentiality of origins, John Hawthorne considers the method of believing p when p can be deduced from the existence of a sperm and egg.[12] Not a method that could easily lead to false beliefs, on that assumption, but if I use it for reasons that have nothing to do with the truth of Kripke's claim, the beliefs it generates fail to count as knowledge.

That the methods I employ in these examples satisfy safety might be questioned. It depends on what they are. If my method is to believe whatever I am hard-wired to believe, or whatever

---

[10] Sosa 2005: 273–4 gives mundane examples of non-adherent knowledge (he calls adherence 'receptivity'); for more systematic objections, see Bird 2003; Kripke 2011: 177–84.

[11] For examples of roughly this shape, see Plantinga 1993a: 195; Sosa 2005: 283; Bedke 2010: §1.1.

[12] Hawthorne 2002: 261–2.

you implant in me a disposition to believe, it may not be safe. I think we can assume, however, that methods are identified psychologically, not by their non-psychological cause.[13] The fact that you induce me to use a certain method mechanically, not through my existing methods, may affect the warrant of my beliefs; but it is not an aspect or constituent of the method I acquire.[14] Different subjects may come to use identical methods in different ways.

None of this shows that safety-of-methods is not a condition of knowing that p. Williamson may be right that, when S knows that p, she knows it on the basis of a method, m, whose output could not easily have been false. Nor is the problem that this condition fails to be sufficient for knowledge. We are not trying to give sufficient conditions for knowing that p. The problem is rather that safety-of-method, even together with adherence, fails to be sufficient for non-accidental truth. What we see in the examples is not just a failure to know, but a failure to know because it is an accident that one's belief is true.

If it is not a failure of safety or adherence, in what does this accident consist? It might be thought that the problem is one of evidence: I do not have adequate grounds for the belief that p, where p is the mathematical truth I believe by innate disposition or through your random interference; nor do I have grounds for the beliefs I deduce from the existence of a sperm and egg. But this is superficial. To begin with, we have to make room for knowledge without evidence. In section 1 of chapter two, I gave an argument from Reductive Epistemology to the prospect of non-evidentially justified belief. Nor can we simply add that the absence of

---

[13] For a view of this topic to which I am broadly sympathetic, see Wedgwood 2002.

[14] This reply is less effective in the coin case, where I choose to associate a particular proposition with heads. The method I use for doing this may not be safe. For this reason, I focus on basic methods, which are not acquired by methods of another kind.

justification, evidential or otherwise, makes for accidental truth. For this proposal is ambiguous. If we mean the absence of doxastic justification sufficient for knowledge, our explanation is trivial. If we mean the absence of propositional justification, it is inadequate. The proposition that p might be one I am entitled to believe without evidence, in the propositional sense, but if I believe it only through your intervention, it is still an accident that my belief is true. If you choose a proposition to implant in me at random, my relation to it does not amount to knowledge, even if the proposition can be non-evidentially known.[15]

More generally, having evidence that supports one's belief, and basing that belief upon one's evidence, does not preclude its accidental truth.[16] Imagine you induce in me the disposition to form beliefs about the future on the basis of certain beliefs about the past. You do so arbitrarily, without regard for the reliability of the disposition or its epistemic rationality. As it happens, the disposition is reliable and, by sheer luck, its premises give inductive evidence for its conclusions. I am disposed to form beliefs on the basis of evidence by which they are propositionally justified. Still, the beliefs I form in this way are at most accidentally true.

[15] This point can be obscured by the use of 'knowledge' for the mere receipt of information. In certain contexts, all we care about is true belief. Thus, in an example due to Hawthorne (2002: §2.1), we ask how many people know the capital of Austria. When we answer this question, we count as knowing the capital all of those who think it is Vienna, regardless of their grounds. (This phenomenon may be one of ambiguity, semantic sensitivity to context, or pragmatically acceptable falsehood; the explanation does not matter here.) Likewise, if you ask how many people know the proposition I was randomly caused to believe, you may want to include me. But this is a distraction. We are interested in knowledge as an epistemic achievement, one of which we can ask, 'How do you know?' This question has no answer when my belief is induced by you.

[16] This follows from the previous paragraph on the assumption that, when I have non-evidential right to believe that all Fs are G, the fact that x is F is evidence that it is G. If my belief that all Fs are G is non-evidentially justified but accidentally true, I do not know that all Fs are G; and I do not know that x is G when I deduce it from this belief together with the fact that x is F. Nor does it help to replace the belief that all Fs are G with the disposition to infer that x is G when I believe that x is F—even though the beliefs produced by this disposition rest on evidence of their truth.

Since my being so disposed has nothing to do with reliability or with the standards of evidence, the disposition is not a source of knowledge. Facts about the content of the disposition and the psychological states to which it is sensitive seem irrelevant to the sense of 'accident' we have been tracking so far.

It might be argued, finally, that the problem in these examples is one of epistemic defeat. In each case, there is a fact about my circumstance—about the origin of my method—knowledge of which destroys the support my beliefs would otherwise have. The presence of this defeater, even when I am not aware of it, conflicts with the attribution of knowledge.[17] My response is not that this is wrong, exactly, but that if it is right, it is consistent with and in fact requires the verdict of accidental truth. The question is: what fact about my circumstance provides the defeating condition? What is it about the origin of my method knowledge of which should undermine my beliefs? As we saw at the beginning of this chapter, although it can seem persuasive, the idea of genetic undermining is difficult to pin down. We may be tempted to cite Coincidence, but we know that this strategy fails. If there is a defeating condition here, isn't it precisely what we are trying to illuminate: the phenomenon of accidental truth? This condition is not helpfully explained by epistemic defeat; if anything, the explanation runs the other way.

In the cases we have considered, one's method is reliable but arbitrary. One's use of this method is random or the product of irrelevant interference. When it generates true beliefs, they fail to count as knowledge because their truth is accidental. If not the absence of justification or the presence of epistemic defeat, in what does the accident consist? This question prompts a natural response. The problem is clear in the recipe for constructing cases: one's method is arbitrary in that one's use of it has nothing to do with its being reliable. In this sense, one's reliability is itself an

---

[17] On knowledge as indefeasibly justified belief, see Klein 1981.

accident. Some authors treat non-accidental reliability as a condition of justified belief.

> Merely happening to be reliable in a given world is not sufficient for the justification of the beliefs yielded by a process, any more than a belief which merely happens to be true can amount to knowledge.... For a connection between a belief-forming process and the truth to be non-accidental is for there to obtain between them a constitutive or explanatory connection. (Majors and Sawyer 2005: 274)

> [Belief]-forming processes can be reliable in some actual or counterfactual environment as a matter of luck, or accidentally, whereas justification-conferring processes should be reliable non-accidentally. (Bedke 2010: 3–4)[18]

My claim will be more modest: that non-accidental reliability of method is a condition of knowledge.[19] This claim has several precedents, cited below. Masahiro Yamada gives an especially close formulation: '[if] it is an accident that one is using a truth-conducive method, then the resulting belief can only be true by accident' (Yamada 2011: 99).[20] More specifically:

> K: When S knows that p, she knows it by a reliable method, and it is no accident that her method is reliable.

This doctrine can be clarified in three ways. First, methods. When knowledge rests on evidence, we can identify one's method with the disposition to believe the truth on relevant grounds, as we did in chapter two. In general, a specification of method should include the psychological states to which one's belief is sensitive: one is disposed to believe p when one has such-and-such beliefs, perceptions, and desires. In the limit case, of a disposition that is not psychologically mediated or conditional, one's method is simply to believe p, or be disposed to form that belief. How

---

[18] For related claims, see Plantinga 1993a: 192, 210; Burge 2003: 507, 534–5.

[19] We will come back to justification in chapter four.

[20] See also Goldman 1986: 51–3 on 'second-order reliability'—though his concern is with the acquisition of methods by learning, where ours is more general.

narrow are the methods that are relevant to K? Should we focus on the disposition to believe a specific proposition, p, on particular grounds, q, or on the general disposition to form beliefs about a certain subject matter in a certain way? These questions recall the so-called 'generality problem' for process reliabilism.[21] If we allow for narrow specification of methods within a standard reliabilist view, the condition of reliability may be too weak. Our situation is, however, different. Even if the methods on which we focus are narrowly circumscribed, and thus reliable, it is a further question whether one's use of reliable methods is accidental. That requirement may still be difficult to meet. For our purposes, it is fine for methods to be narrow. The only constraint is that the conditions to which they are sensitive be 'proportional' to their effects: one is disposed to believe p in circumstance C, and one does not have this disposition merely in virtue of being disposed to believe p in some determinable circumstance, $C^\star$, of which C is a determinate. The specific content of the input must be relevant to what one believes.[22] Although methods can be narrow, they can also be general. But even here there are some constraints. When a method applies to many beliefs, it is not simply a conjunction of dispositions. It must be unified, and its unity lies in the common contents of the attitudes on which it rests. Going by how things look is a general method; an arbitrary list of inputs and outputs is not.

Second, when is reliability an accident? We are interested in the connection or correlation between two facts: that S uses m and that m is a reliable way to form beliefs. It is this conjunction that must be no accident. A modal or safety interpretation is too weak to capture this idea: it is not enough that m is reliable in most nearby worlds in which S uses it or that it could not easily yield a false belief. That would be true if m is necessarily reliable, even

[21] Feldman 1985.
[22] On proportionality in mental causation, see Yablo 1992.

though its reliability is unrelated to S. What we need is an *explanatory* connection: a connection between the reliability of *m* and the fact that S is disposed to use it. Three kinds of 'because' may be relevant here: efficient, final, and formal.[23] Perhaps S uses *m* because it is reliable or its reliability follows from the etiology of its use; perhaps these factors have a common cause. Perhaps S uses *m* for the sake of forming true beliefs: it is the function of *m* to be reliable and the connection is teleological. Perhaps the conjunction is constitutively explained. A constitutive account of *x* is an account of its nature, or what it is to be that thing: in Aristotelian terms, its essence or formal cause.[24] A constitutive explanation of *p* and *q* is one in which *p* follows from *q* together with truths of this kind. Thus the reliability of *m* might follow from what it is for that method to be used by S. (These possibilities are quite abstract; they will be illustrated shortly.)

Those who recognize K, or something like it, often emphasize just one of these forms. Thus Matthew Bedke writes: 'a given process is non-accidentally reliable in a justification-relevant way if and when that process is reliable *because of its etiology*' (Bedke 2010: 4).[25] Alvin Plantinga insists, as a condition of knowledge, that one's method be reliable and have reliability as its 'proper function': '[what] confers warrant is one's cognitive faculties working properly, or working according to the design plan *insofar as that segment of the design plan is aimed at producing true beliefs*' (Plantinga 1993b: 16).[26] And according to Tyler Burge, in a treatment of perceptual warrant, '[reliable] connections to the world

---

[23] These are three of Aristotle's 'four causes'; material causation seems irrelevant to K.

[24] The idea of nature or essence has been rehabilitated in recent work by Kit Fine (see Fine 1994); for discussion of this, and much else in the area, I am indebted to Cian Dorr.

[25] Though Bedke also cites some teleological views (Bedke 2010: 4–5).

[26] For Plantinga, the 'design plan' is a matter of divine creation (Plantinga 1993b: Ch. 11). For others, it can be naturalized; see, for instance, Millikan 1984.

that are accidental relative to the conditions that individuate the individual's perceptual states make no contribution to epistemic entitlement' (Burge 2003: 535).[27] My view is ecumenical: it allows for K to be satisfied in any of these ways. What is required is an explanatory connection between the use of S by m and its being reliable, where the explanation may be formal, final, or efficient.

A final clarification is that K may not exhaust the condition of non-accidental truth. It may not deal with every Gettier case, or explain why one cannot know that one's lottery ticket will lose by the reliable method of discounting the improbable—both phenomena that have been thought to involve accidentally true belief. There may be more to the no-accident condition than K reveals. What matters for our purposes is not that K is a complete account of knowledge, or of its non-accidental character, but simply that it is true. Why believe this? In part because K solves the problems for safety and adherence above: it explains what is accidental about the truth of my beliefs in the cases I described. In part because it unifies the insights of related views. Finally, as I will argue in section 3, because K explains why there is a problem of scepticism in ethics if the facts are irreducible, inert, and constitutively independent of us. While most suspect some difficulty here, the previous chapters failed to articulate what it is. That is what K will help us to do.

2. REFLECTION, INDUCTION, PERCEPTION

Before we turn to that project, I pause to address a pre-emptive concern: that K excludes too much. The fear is that K makes trouble in ethics only at the cost of threatening knowledge elsewhere. In particular, there is a puzzle about inductive and

---

[27] See also Majors and Sawyer 2005: 274, quoted in the text above; Bealer 1999 on 'modal reliabilism'; and Peacocke 2004.

explanatory inference, in light of K: how could it be anything but luck that the standards of 'best explanation' we are disposed to employ reliably track the truth? And there is a puzzle in the epistemology of a priori knowledge. If we are not affected by the relevant facts, what could explain the reliability of our beliefs? In each case, there is a question how to meet the demands of K.

The issues here are delicate. If K is hard to satisfy, should we doubt its truth, or embrace the difficulties? It might be thought a virtue of K that it locates the deepest roots of a priori or inductive scepticism. That is in fact my view: the truth of K is a constraint on knowledge in these areas, but it is a constraint that can be met. While an adequate treatment would take us far afield, it will be useful to sketch the strategies available to the anti-sceptic. As well as reassuring us about K, this sketch will set the set the terms for our treatment of ethical knowledge. It will provide a sense of the ways in which knowledge can be explained, and the challenge of doing so in the ethical case.

Consider first the possibility of non-empirical knowledge, including knowledge of logical and analytic truths. If we are reliable about these topics, what explains this fact? A tempting view is that such knowledge turns on the nature of concept-possession. Suppose that part of what it is to possess a given concept is that one's disposition to believe things about the application of this concept, not on the basis of evidence but of immediate reflection, be sufficient reliable: it generates mostly true beliefs. As will see, this principle is too strong; but it is helpful to begin with the simplest view. Suppose, then, that S is disposed to believe some array of propositions involving concept C on the basis of immediate reflection. It follows from this fact, and from the principle above, that this disposition is reliable. If we equate the disposition with a method of belief-formation, m, this picture is enough to satisfy K. Its conjunction is constitutively explained: that

S uses m entails that m is reliable through the nature of the facts involved.[28]

This conception differs in important ways from a more familiar appeal to meaning-constitution. According to the more familiar view, it is a condition of possessing concept C that one be disposed to use some method, m, in making inferences to and from claims in which C appears. It follows, allegedly, that the use of m is epistemically rational.[29] A standard objection cites so-called 'defective concepts', like *Boche*, whose possession involves thinking in irrational ways.[30] It is a condition of having the concept, *Boche*, the story goes, that one be disposed to infer from x is German to x is Boche, and from x is Boche to x is cruel. This pattern of inference is not thereby justified. One response is to dispute the theory of pejorative concepts: I am pretty sure I have the concept *Boche*, since I understand what is being said by people who use it; but I have no disposition at all to infer in these unfortunate ways.[31] We need not pursue this here. Unlike the more familiar appeal to meaning-constitution, the theory of a priori knowledge above allows for concepts whose possession turns on defective inference or belief. What the theory claims, as a condition of concept-possession, is not that one use a particular method in making inferences that exploit that concept, or that this method be rational, but that one's disposition to believe things about the application of the concept, not on the basis of evidence, be sufficiently reliable. *Boche* would be in conflict with this claim only if those who have the concept *Boche* are disposed not only to make the inferences in question, and so to believe that Germans are cruel, but to hold this belief on the basis of immediate reflection. But this is not the case. When users of *Boche* assert

[28] For a similar approach to the a priori, see Bealer 1999, though he cites intuitions as intellectual seemings where I have groundless beliefs.
[29] For ideas in this vicinity, see Peacocke 1993, 2004: Ch. 6; Boghossian 1996, 2003.
[30] The example is due to Dummett 1973: 454; it is discussed in Boghossian 2003.
[31] For similar doubts, see Williamson 2003: §II.

that Germans are cruel, they give reasons, however bad ones, for their belief.

Nor can we simply stipulate otherwise. As Williamson insists, there is no guarantee that an arbitrary set of rules or methods will define a genuine thought.[32] In our terms: there is no guarantee that a concept corresponds to just any disposition to believe. The most difficult cases turn not on stipulation, but on actual concepts, like *set*, about which we have false but arguably groundless beliefs. How much of a problem do such concepts raise? While we may be disposed to accept naïve comprehension without evidence, I doubt that this is a condition for possessing the concept *set*. More significantly, it is no part of the present theory that if we are disposed to accept something on the basis of reflection, it is true, or that if its truth is analytic, we are disposed to accept it. The condition is one of sufficient reliability, and while there are difficult questions about degrees of reliability and their measurement, an adequate conception should allow for the present case. Believing in naïve comprehension is consistent with being reliable enough in one's beliefs to know other set-theoretic truths.

In a searching discussion of these topics, Paul Horwich contrasts two ways in which we might draw on the methods involved in concept-possession.[33] On the first, we hold that using m is a condition of possessing a concept, and that its use is therefore rational. This is what I have called 'the familiar view'. On the second, we hold that possession of the concept turns on the reliability of m, and this is what justifies its use. Horwich contends that the first approach is flawed, and that the second is a form of reliabilism on which the fact that m is meaning-constituting plays no essential role. As he puts it:

[Two] separate explanatory arrows go directly from the truth-theoretic correctness of [the method] to, on the one hand, its being justified and,

---

[32] Williamson 2003: §III.
[33] Horwich 2005: §9.

on the other hand, to its constituting a meaning. There is no explanatory arrow from its constituting a meaning to its being justified. (Horwich 2005: 156)[34]

The need for an explanation of reliability that satisfies K explains why meaning-constitution is not redundant in the way that Horwich fears. On the view that we are considering, possession of a concept turns on the reliability of one's disposition to groundless belief. Although the nature of concept-possession does not explain why S believes the particular things he does, it allows us to explain, in constitutive terms, the crucial connection, between the fact that m is reliable and the fact that S uses m. Our epistemology demands not just reliability of methods, but that it be no accident that one's method is reliable. It is this further demand, which goes beyond reliabilism, that meaning-constitution meets.

There is a final issue to confront. On the explanation of reliability I have sketched, part of what it is to have a given concept is that one's disposition to believe things about the application of this concept, not on the basis of evidence but of immediate reflection, be sufficiently reliable. Is this claim actually true? It is in certain ways logically weak. It need not apply to every concept, only to concepts through which there is a priori knowledge. Nor does it imply that, in possessing a concept, one is disposed to believe without evidence some significant range of propositions, only that, if you are, most of what you are disposed to believe is true. Still, the claim may ask too much. Is it required in possessing an ordinary concept—*number, frog, electron*—that one be reliable in one's groundless beliefs? Most likely not. As Tyler Burge observed in a well-known thought-experiment, it is possible to grasp the concept *arthritis* while being ignorant of elementary facts about the condition.[35] Extending his point: if I am fluent speaker of English, I can make assertions and form beliefs about such things

---

[34] See also Horwich 2005: 164–5.
[35] Burge 1979.

as numbers, frogs, and electrons, using these words, even if I am pervasively mistaken in the groundless beliefs I form. What I believe without evidence about numbers, frogs, electrons, may be largely incorrect.[36] If this is right, our account of a priori knowledge is flawed.

The account can be repaired. Let us admit that possession-conditions for concepts are often social, not individual. The demand for reliability survives, in mediated form: part of what it is to possess a concept C is to belong to a conceptual or linguistic community whose disposition to believe things about the application of C, not on the basis of evidence, is sufficiently reliable. Call this disposition m, and suppose that S uses m because the community does.[37] That the community uses m is a generic claim, consistent with exceptions, not a universal generalization. It follows from this claim, and from the nature of concept-possession, that m is a reliable method. This structure is enough to satisfy K: we have an explanation of why S uses m that entails its reliability through the nature of the facts involved. At the same time, we allow for individuals who grasp the concept in question, being part of the same linguistic community, but whose dispositions lead them to mostly false beliefs.

So much for a priori knowledge. Nothing in this account restricts its scope to analytic truths or truths of logic. There is room for a broader epistemology of numbers and possible worlds. We will not pursue those issues here. Instead, we turn to knowledge by inductive and explanatory inference. Here a constitutive explanation of reliability seems wrong. It is not a condition of thought about the subject matter of such inference, or of thought as such, that one's inductive and explanatory methods be reliable

---

[36] For extensions in this spirit, see Burge 1986; Williamson 2003, 2007: Ch. 4.

[37] Or did. What matters is the community whose use explains one's possession of the concept; and this community may be historical.

in the world that one inhabits.[38] It is not impossible to infer in unreliable ways. How, then, can such knowledge satisfy K?

We have methods of inductive and explanatory inference that are hard to specify but relatively disciplined and more or less widely shared. What explains their reliability? An obvious thought is that reliable inference is an evolutionary advantage, and that our methods evolved by natural selection.[39] The disposition to use these methods is innate, though its manifestation is contingent, and its presence is explained by the methods' reliability. Tempting though it is, there are three main problems with this approach. First, is it clear that our methods of inductive and explanatory inference are, in the relevant sense, innate? Second, while selection might explain our reliability about facts that are relevant to survival and reproduction, what explains our reliability in the more speculative realms to which inference is now applied? Third, while it may explain the properties of populations, how can selection explain individual traits? How can it relate the fact that m is reliable to its use by a particular subject, S? I will argue that the first two problems can be solved; the third requires a shift from prior causation to teleology.

On the question of innateness: while it may not be true that specific methods of inquiry are innate, that is not required for the present approach. It is enough that there are innate restrictions on learning through which we are disposed to acquire more or less reliable inductive and explanatory methods, methods that are otherwise unconstrained.[40] Nor do the methods we begin with or acquire need to be reliable to a high degree, just reliable enough to

[38] Though compare a generalized appeal to interpretive charity, of the kind invoked by Davidson 1983 or Williamson 2007: Ch. 8.

[39] 'Creatures inveterately wrong in their inductions have a pathetic but praiseworthy tendency to die before reproducing their kind' (Quine 1969: 125–6). This thought does not assume that selection always favours more reliable methods, or that its products are optimally designed. It is thus immune to the objections of Stephen Stich (1990: §§3.2–3.3).

[40] See Goldman 1986 on the object of 'primary epistemology'.

give us knowledge with which their performance can be improved. These assumptions could in principle be denied, but they are not especially strong.

The other problems have been discussed by Elliott Sober, to differing effect. On the second issue, about the extent of reliability to be explained, Sober notes that the most efficient cognitive mechanism for reliability about the facts that matter to fitness may be one that is reliable elsewhere.[41] If so, natural selection would favour general reliability by opposing inefficiency in cognitive means. It is therefore not a mystery how reliable methods have evolved. From our point of view, the weakness of this response is that it makes the broader reliability of inductive and explanatory inference a side-effect or spandrel. Their being generally reliable is a consequence of natural selection, but does not itself play an explanatory role. We do not use these methods because they are generally reliable, but because they are efficient mechanisms for reliability in a more local realm. This fact is not enough to satisfy K.

The solution, I think, is to find a common cause. Roughly put: the laws of nature that make inductive and explanatory inference reliable, in general, explain their reliability in the circumstances of selection, which in turn explains why their use evolved. There is thus an explanation of how we came to use these methods that entails their reliability elsewhere. This account relies on controversial claims: that regularities can be explained by laws of nature; and that there is a common structure behind the reliability of explanatory inference in, say, tracking predators, and in forming beliefs about unobservable facts. Without these premises, the explanation fails. Are they defensible? I think so, though I will not defend them here. It is worth noting that similar problems arise for past and future reliability. Someone might object that selection cannot explain the future reliability of our methods

[41] Sober 1981.

because it is irrelevant to their evolution. Only past reliability counts. Again, the solution is to find a common cause. Past and future reliability are explained by the same laws of nature. If that were not the case, if they were truly independent, our reliability about the future would be a matter of inexplicable luck. Even here, we need the common explanation of regularities by laws.

According to the third objection, natural selection can explain only facts about populations, not individual traits, and so not the use of reliable methods by S. In *The Nature of Selection*, Sober presses this argument by comparison.[42] Selection works by eliminating individuals with certain traits, not by affecting their traits directly. Consider a class that admits only children who can read at third-grade level. This fact about selection will explain why the population of the class consists of children who can read at least that well. It does nothing to explain why any particular child can read at third-grade level, a fact that is wholly independent of the selective constraint. Sober holds that the same is true of natural selection: it can explain why a population is wholly or predominantly F; it does not explain why any member of that population has the traits it does. Thus, even if the reliability of *m* explains, through selection, why *m* is used by the population at large, it cannot explain why S uses *m*, and cannot help to satisfy K.

We might be puzzled by this view. Imagine a population of organisms that reproduce by mating. If natural selection explains why the population is predominantly and heritably F, won't that explain why S's parents happened to mate with an F individual, and thus why S is F? In response, we should distinguish two objects of explanation: the fact that a parent had an offspring who is F; and the fact that S is F. Natural selection can explain the former, by making it more probable; but if S has its parents essentially, this won't affect the probability of the latter. As Mohan Matthen writes, 'when you pin down these two individuals, the actual

    [42] Sober 1984: §5.2.

parents, you have screened out the very influence [on the mating population] that previous selection has' (Matthen 1999: 147).[43]

The solution to this problem is to shift attention from the etiology of individual traits to their biological function. Facts about the selective benefits of reliable inference and their role in its evolution may not explain why an individual came to use method m, but they may be sufficient for the method to have reliability as its final cause. As the function of the heart is to pump blood around the body, so we use method m for the sake of believing the truth. While I won't attempt a theory of biological function, and while existing theories differ in significant ways, almost all agree that when the function of the F in a certain population is to ϕ, the F is present in that population, or is disposed to be there, in part because it ϕs.[44] Etiological claims like those above are therefore relevant to function or teleology. There is reason to hope for a teleological account of inductive and explanatory knowledge on which it is the function of our methods of inference to generate true beliefs. If this connection holds, that is enough to satisfy K.

---

[43] Matthen goes on to deny the essentiality of parental origins, so as to block the argument in the text (Matthen 1999: §6). I won't pursue that strategy here.

[44] For views that appeal to past selection, see Millikan 1989, Neander 1991, Godfrey-Smith 1994. Even dispositional views, like that of Bigelow and Pargetter 1987, require that the functional activities of a trait explain, or be able to explain, its future persistence. For a broader etiological approach, which allows for artefacts and divine creation, as well as evolution by selection, see Wright 1973, 1976. A problem for all these views is that traits may ensure their own persistence even though they fail to benefit their subjects. Such traits appear to have no function. (Bedau 1991 and Manning 1997: 74–5 give examples drawn from nature; Plantinga 1993b: 203–4 invents some a priori.) Accordingly, a more plausible view would hold that the function of the F in a certain population is to ϕ when the F is present in that population in part because it ϕs, only if the explanation of its presence turns on benefits of some kind. More radical critiques derive from Alvin Plantinga (1993b: Ch. 11), who takes a theistic line; and from Michael Thompson (2008: Part One) and Philippa Foot (2001: Ch. 2–3). In my view, there is room for a synthesis of these ideas; but I cannot attempt that here. Related questions, about human nature and its ethical import, will be pursued in chapter four.

Let me stress at once that this account is hypothetical. It rests on speculative claims about the role of laws in explanation, and about the evolution and development of cognitive traits. The point of presenting it is not to solve the problem of scientific knowledge, a task that is well beyond our scope, but to suggest that it can in principle be solved. That the problem is difficult reflects a puzzle in the epistemology of inductive and explanatory inference. It gives us little reason to doubt the truth of K.[45]

To end this section, I address, though briefly, knowledge by perception. Here the problem is not whether K is satisfied, but how. I won't attempt to settle this question, but I will sketch some possibilities. The first is teleological: it echoes our account of inductive knowledge. If the perceptual systems that issue in appearance, and our disposition to trust them, evolved because they are sufficiently reliable, it may be the function of trusting appearances to generate true beliefs. A second view is constitutive: it cites connections of the sort that account for a priori knowledge. Here we find those who appeal to externalism about perceptual content, holding that perception necessarily represents the objects and conditions it tracks, at least in its proper environment.[46] That it is reliable in this environment is constitutively explained: it is not a contingent fact. While this view is in some ways tempting, the version of externalism required to satisfy K is relatively strong. It must follow from the fact that S forms perceptual beliefs, and from the nature of perceptual content, that her method is reliable,

---

[45] If inductive knowledge is teleological and teleology depends on history, it follows that 'Swampman', who springs into existence instantaneously, cannot know by inductive inference: his inductive beliefs are accidentally true. It does not follow, however, that Swampman knows nothing, since introspective, a priori, and even perceptual knowledge may be explained in other ways. (Compare Sosa 1993: 56–7, whose objection to Plantinga rests on the stronger claim.) What is more, on dispositional theories of function, like that of Bigelow and Pargetter (1987), Swampman's use of inductive inference may be functional after all.

[46] For instance: Burge 2003; Peacocke 2004: Chs. 2–3; Majors and Sawyer 2005; Wedgwood 2007: 230–2.

period; reliability in some favoured circumstance is not enough. Although it is controversial, this theory of perceptual content might be true.[47] Its defence would turn on the relative weakness of dispositional claims. Our perceptual states may be disposed to reveal the truth even if they are frequently prevented, as a glass may be disposed to break when struck even though it is carefully packed.[48] Finally, we might reject the description of methods on which perceptual beliefs rest on appearance, as such. If our method is to believe that p when we perceive it veridically, not when it seems to be the case, the claim that our method is reliable, period, not just in our proper environment, is easier to defend.[49] Those who appeal to factive mental states as evidence can thus give a constitutive explanation of reliability without concluding that appearances are disposed to be veridical, as such.

If this is right, there are several ways in which perceptual knowledge could conform to K. We need not decide between them here. More generally, the condition of knowledge that one's reliability be no accident—that it have an explanation by final, formal, or efficient cause—does not force a sceptical result. At least in principle, it allows for knowledge by ordinary means, a priori, inductive, and perceptual. Though this is not an argument for K, it pre-empts a possible objection. K is not excessively strong. When S knows that p, she knows it by a reliable method, and her reliability is no accident. As we will see, this condition can be satisfied in ethics only if there is a constitutive connection between fact and belief.

---

[47] It is proposed by Nico Silins (forthcoming: §3.2), who suggests that 'one can rewrite Burge's overall account of perceptual entitlement in terms of essentialist reliability' and that this account 'is plausibly at least as good as his own'. Silins does not himself accept the essentialist view.

[48] More on dispositions below.

[49] On veridical perception as the basis of belief, see McDowell 2008. Williamson argues that methods of belief-formation can appeal to factive states; see Williamson 2000: 178–81. These ideas are related to Burge on constitutive reliability in Silins forthcoming: §3.2.

3. THE PROBLEM OF ETHICAL KNOWLEDGE

Suppose, instead, that the facts in ethics are constitutively independent of us. Our attitudes do not figure in an account of what it is for there to be a reason for A to ϕ or what it is for an action to be right or wrong. Nor does reliability about these facts belong to the nature of ethical belief, as in our schematic account of a priori knowledge. For simplicity, let us begin with the austere but influential view on which these claims are accompanied by a non-reductive metaphysics of reasons, right and wrong, and by a confession of causal impotence. At least the primary ethical facts are wholly irreducible and causally inert.[50] It is an arresting vision, inspiring to some, disturbing to others. A common complaint is epistemological. This 'Moorean' view, the objection runs, must be allied with an implausible intuitionism, on which we are non-causally sensitive to transcendent facts. How to make sense of this? But without such sensitivity, can it be more than a coincidence that our beliefs are true? We saw in the previous chapter that one interpretation of this challenge is flawed. There is no problem of coincidence, as such, nor does its solution turn on mysterious non-causal interaction with values. It can be solved by getting clear on the structure of justification for ethical belief. But a problem remains, about the satisfaction of K. If ethical facts are irreducible and causally inert, and if there is no constitutive connection between our attitudes and the facts, our reliability about these facts is bound to be accidental. Consider the ways in which it could be explained. Do I form beliefs in ethics using m because it is a reliable method? No. Though we may be able to explain why we use m instead of other methods, perhaps in terms of natural selection, its being reliable about these causally impotent facts

---

[50] For views of this kind, see Moore 1903; Ross 1930; Nagel 1986: Ch. 8; Dworkin 1996; Parfit 1997, 2006, 2011; Hampton 1998; Scanlon 1998: 55–72; Shafer-Landau 2003; Enoch 2010.

can play no role in its etiology. Since functions turn on etiologies of this kind, or on their being possible, this point precludes an explanation by final cause. Finally, since the facts are constitutively independent of our beliefs, our reliability cannot be constitutively explained. Our assumptions leave no room for the satisfaction of K by efficient, final, or formal cause. They make ethical knowledge impossible.

Perhaps surprisingly, the problem is not confined to non-reductive views.[51] Taken by itself, Reductionism does nothing to help. For the reductionist, ethical properties can be non-ethically specified: we can say what it is to have each property without using ethical concepts. Understood in this way, ethical properties may well have causal powers. To take a crude example, if being right is maximizing pleasure, and the fact that something maximizes pleasure explains why I think it is right, then I believe it is right because it is. Perhaps I am disposed to believe an action right whenever I think it maximizes pleasure, and I am responsive to the causing of pleasure and pain. There is no mystery here about the mechanism of reliability. But this is not enough to satisfy K. For that, we need an explanation of my reliability on which it is no accident. My being disposed to believe an action right when it maximizes pleasure must have something to do with the fact that maximizing pleasure makes an action right. For the reductionist, the latter fact rests on the constitution of right and wrong: for an action to be right just is for it to maximize pleasure. That is why my disposition is reliable. The problem is that, while this identity entails that I am reliable, and while it gives causal powers to an action's being right, the fact behind my reliability—that being right is maximizing pleasure—remains inert, and cannot explain the method I use. This theoretical identity is not a contingent truth or a part of the causal order. I am not disposed to believe an

---

[51] Street makes a parallel claim about Coincidence (Street 2006: 139–41).

action right when it maximizes pleasure because being right is maximizing pleasure: the condition in K has not been met.

The argument of the previous paragraph assumes that the method relevant to K is inferential: I infer that an act is right from the belief that it maximizes pleasure. Matters are more complicated if, instead of making this inference, I am disposed to go directly from evidence that an act will maximize pleasure to the belief that it is right, or if my belief that it is right to act in certain ways does not depend on evidence but its etiology turns on the fact that those ways of acting maximize pleasure.[52] In each case, my reliability corresponds to a contingent fact—that this evidence is a reliable guide to what maximizes pleasure, that these ways of acting do so—not a necessary truth. In principle, such facts could explain my methods, entailing their reliability through the nature of the facts involved. But it would be absurd to think that our capacity for ethical knowledge depends on proceeding in these elusive ways, or that it would vanish if, instead of going directly from evidence to ethical belief, I made explicit the intermediate step (that this act maximizes pleasure), or instead of simply believing that certain ways of acting are right, I understood why! It follows that the mere truth of Reductionism does not explain the possibility of ethical knowledge. That the inferential method is reliable—since being right is maximizing pleasure—cannot explain my use of it by final or efficient cause. Nor does it help to replace this inference with more direct paths to ethical belief, since ethical knowledge would be possible even if it had an inferential structure. So long as we maintain the constitutive independence of fact and belief, the sceptical problem remains.

At this stage, we can relax the assumption of causal impotence in non-reductive views. Let facts about reasons, right and wrong,

---

[52] For reasons given in chapter one, I set aside the prospect of a perceptual epistemology.

be irreducible but causally effective.[53] This will make progress with K only if the reliability of our methods plays a role in explaining why we use them. It is not enough that particular facts, about particular acts and agents, cause particular beliefs. We need to explain why I am disposed to form those beliefs in reliable ways. For the non-evidential theorist, we need ethical principles to explain why I am disposed to believe them. In Reductive Epistemology, we need the fact that if x is N then x is E to explain why I am disposed to believe that x is E when I have evidence that x is N. On this point, however, the evolutionary sceptics are right.[54] There is no explanation of either kind, no credible story to tell about the origin of our evaluative methods or dispositions on which they are explained by irreducible relations between ethical properties and the facts on which they supervene. Though natural selection may explain why we use m instead of other methods, the principles that relate non-ethical properties to ethical facts, and so make m reliable, play no explanatory role.

There is a possible exception to these claims. I have been considering explanations of reliability that proceed in secular terms, citing the evolution of ethical belief. Such explanations are speculative, but even if they work, they do not help to satisfy K. Things look different if we turn to God. Assuming God can know the truth in ethics, even if it is irreducible, he may create in us, or some of us, reliable dispositions.[55] On this account, ethical principles *can* explain how we are disposed to form true beliefs. This is, I think, the only hope for ethical knowledge if the facts are constitutively independent of us. Some may find in it an argument for the existence of God, or for his ethical significance. Those topics are too vast to be embarked on here. They were ignored by earlier formulations, and will be ignored

---

[53] As they are according to Graham Oddie and Ralph Wedgwood (Oddie 2005: Ch. 7; Wedgwood 2007: Ch. 8).

[54] Street 2006: 125–30; Joyce 2006: Ch. 6.

[55] See Adams 1999: 363–72.

below.[56] On the assumption of atheism, our conclusion is this: so long as we hold in place the constitutive independence of fact and belief, it does not matter whether Reductionism is true, or whether facts about reasons, right and wrong have causal powers; there is no way to meet the demand for non-accidental reliability as a condition of knowledge. If ethical knowledge is possible, the facts in ethics are constitutively bound to us.

Since I know that torture is wrong, that courage is a virtue, that there is reason to care about people other than oneself, and since I think you know it, too, constitutive independence has to go. Ethical knowledge is possible, and its possibility is explained by the constitutive connection of our attitudes with the facts. As I have stressed before, it does not follow from this connection that ethical facts are constituted by us. The explanation could run the other way, from fact to belief, as it did in our account of a priori knowledge. In the rest of this chapter, I explore constitutive explanations of reliability in ethical belief. Is ethical knowledge just another case of knowledge by reflection, explained by some development of the strategy in section 2? Should we adopt a constructivist view? I will argue that there are serious problems either way. The deepest challenge to knowledge in ethics is how to connect our attitudes with the facts, so as to explain reliability, without predicting more convergence in belief than it is credible to expect.

Although I have emphasized the possibility of alternative views, and will do so again, ethical constructivism is perhaps the most obvious approach to K. I call 'constructivist' views on which the truth of ethical propositions is explained in terms of our attitudes towards them.[57] For the sake of being definite, I will focus on judgements of virtue, and begin with the simplest possible claim.

---

[56] We return to them, briefly, in chapter four.

[57] Constructivism in this sense is distinct from 'constitutivism' or what I have elsewhere called 'ethical rationalism', on which the standards of practical reason derive from the nature of agency. Christine Korsgaard's treatment of constructivism

UNQUALIFIED CONSTRUCTIVISM: For a trait to be a virtue is for us to be disposed to think it is.

No doubt we are disposed to think different things in different circumstances. The simple view asks what we are disposed to believe without qualification, and lets the facts about virtue turn on how just anyone is disposed. More plausible theories would cite our disposition to believe that something is a virtue in conditions of non-ethical information, ideal reflection, and the like.[58] We will come back to these conditions below. What matters now is that the unqualified constructivist can satisfy K. If S is disposed to believe that *a*, *b*, *c* are virtues, it follows from the nature of virtue that they are. Where *m* is the disposition in question, it is no accident that S uses *m* and that *m* is reliable. The conjunction is constitutively explained.

Although her view is more subtle than this, and although she is concerned with Coincidence, not K, Street's constructivism runs on similar lines.[59] For Street, 'the fact that X is a reason for A to Y is constituted by the fact that the judgment that X is a reason (for A) to Y withstands scrutiny from the standpoint of A's other judgments about reasons' (Street ms.: §6). This is meant to explain the correlation between A's beliefs about reasons and the facts about what there is reason for her to do, on the assumption that A tends to form beliefs about reasons that withstand scrutiny from one another's point of view. There may appear to be a contrast between Street's constructivism and the constructivist schema above, in that the former speaks to reasons *for* A, connecting them with A's beliefs. It does not explicitly claim that reasons for

as an alternative to realism runs together or combines the two: her 'constructivist' is also a constitutivist (see, especially, Korsgaard 2003). But while they are compatible, these views are not the same. From the standpoint of epistemology, what matters is the connection of fact with belief, not intentional action: constructivism, not ethical rationalism. I criticize rationalism, on action-theoretic grounds, in Setiya 2007.

[58] For discussion, see Lewis 1989: 121–6; Street 2008: §7.
[59] Street 2006, 2008, ms.

others are constituted by facts about the judgements that withstand scrutiny from A's evaluative standpoint, or that reasons for A are constituted by facts about the judgements that withstand scrutiny from the standpoint of anyone else. But this appearance must deceive if Street's constructivism is to explain the reliability of A's beliefs about other people's reasons or their beliefs about his. And it is not what Street intends. Instead, her view is that constructivism and only constructivism 'withstands scrutiny from within the standpoint of *every agent's* normative commitments' because it alone makes room for ethical knowledge. Thus, although she is sceptical of 'Kantian antirealism', according to which a commitment to *moral* reasons follows 'from within every practical point of view...there is one strong, substantive conclusion about our reasons [that does follow], namely constructivism itself ' (Street ms.: §12). Reflective scrutiny from the standpoint of our initial normative commitments would lead us to agree that an agent's reasons are constituted by the judgements that withstand scrutiny from her practical point of view, and so to agree about reasons, as such. What someone thinks about anyone's reasons (at least if her beliefs withstand mutual scrutiny) tends to be true.

The parenthetic clause indicates that Street's constructivism is not unqualified: there is a special condition under which our judgements correlate with the facts. Before I turn to the complications induced by this, I take issue with Street's more general claim, that *only* constructivists can explain the coincidence of ethical fact and belief. Transposed from Coincidence to K: only if the facts are constituted by attitudes we are disposed to have under some condition or other can our reliability in ethics be no accident. We already know that this is not the case. Although I argued, above, that ethical knowledge turns on the failure of constitutive independence, it is possible for facts that are both irreducible and causally inert to satisfy K. The direction of constitution may go the other way. Think back to our treatment of a priori knowledge in section 2. If part of what it is to possess a concept is that one's non-evidential methods be sufficiently reliable, one's reliability in using these methods is no accident. The non-reductionist in ethics may adopt a similar view.

EXTERNALISM: Part of what it is to have the concept of ethical virtue is to be such that one's method for identifying traits as virtues is sufficiently reliable.

If S uses m to identify virtues, it follows that she has the concept of ethical virtue, and it follows from this fact, and from the nature of concept-possession, that m is a reliable method. K is met by constitutive explanation.

Ralph Wedgwood stands to Externalism roughly as Street stands to the unqualified version of constructivism: his view is more subtle, but similar in approach.[60] Wedgwood draws on a certain reading of the 'normativity of the intentional'. For Wedgwood, what it is to possess a concept, or to be capable of an attitude-type, is to be disposed to conform to basic principles of rationality that govern the use of that concept or the instantiation of that attitude.[61] For each concept or attitude, some principle of rationality plays this constitutive role. Rationality in general ensures that one's use of a concept or instantiation of an attitude is likely to be correct. For our purposes, likelihood may be read in dispositional terms.[62] Thus, it follows from the normativity of the intentional that we are disposed to use concepts correctly, and to instantiate attitudes only when it is correct to do so. Wedgwood's position is complicated in ways that impede the satisfaction of K. For one thing, he takes the basic principle of rationality that

---

[60] I am thinking in particular of Wedgwood 2007.

[61] Wedgwood 2007: Ch. 7; also 234–6. For a similar view, see Peacocke 2004: Chs. 7–8. Michael Smith defends a reductive or naturalized version of the same approach; see, especially, Smith 2010.

[62] For Wedgwood's remarks on rationality, correctness, and likelihood, see Wedgwood 2007: 156, 227–8, 239–40.

governs the primary ethical concept, *ought*, to be 'normative judgement internalism', according to which it is irrational not to intend what one thinks one ought to do.[63] He thus denies that dispositions governing the ground or formation of ethical beliefs, as opposed to their volitional upshot, are essential to the possession of this concept.[64] This makes it harder to derive a disposition to believe the truth from the nature of ethical thought. A second complication is that, alongside the disposition to be rational involved in possessing a concept or attitude, Wedgwood allows that we may have competing dispositions which 'mask' its operation.[65] One need not be disposed to get things right, all told. Again, this tends to frustrate the satisfaction of K.[66] Wedgwood's epistemological project is in any case different from ours: not to explain how knowledge is possible, but how ethical beliefs can be rational, on a certain conception of epistemic rationality.[67] Despite all this, Wedgwood's view belongs to the externalist family in giving a constitutive account of ethical belief that ties it to the facts. A connection of this kind could meet the condition of non-accidental truth for ethical knowledge with a non-reductive view of ethical facts.

In filling out the range of possibilities, we should note that while Externalism is consistent with non-reductionism, it does not require it. I argued above that Reductionism alone is not enough to satisfy K. But reductionists can be externalists, too. And as it happens, most reductionists give semantic accounts of ethical concepts on which our methods for applying them are bound up with the facts. In the 'Cornell realism' of Richard Boyd and David Brink, ethical concepts refer to the properties tracked

---

[63] Wedgwood 2007: 24–7, 97.
[64] Wedgwood 2007: 105–6.
[65] See, especially, Wedgwood 2007: 165, 237.
[66] And it is in any case puzzling: can a disposition be masked by an enduring disposition of the very same thing? More on this to come.
[67] Wedgwood, 2007: 227–32.

by, or causally responsible for, our modes of ethical inquiry.[68] Frank Jackson argues for a form of 'moral functionalism' on which the content of ethical concepts is fixed by the platitudes governing their use.[69] Either way, it follows from the nature of ethical thought that our methods of belief-formation are more or less reliable.

We should be struck, at this point, by an emerging consensus among the standard theories of ethical truth. Despite their differences, these views address the problem of ethical knowledge by giving accounts of ethical fact and belief on which their constitutive connection is enough to satisfy K. Although their authors do not articulate K, as such, its plausibility is confirmed by this agreement. If the facts are constituted by our dispositions to believe, or our beliefs in part by a tendency to match the facts, it need not be an accident when those beliefs are true.

Despite this consensus, I do not think we can accept such views. What kills their plausibility is the very implication with which they conform to K. At least in the simple forms above, these views imply that we are disposed to believe the truth. Specifically: anyone who has the concept of virtue is disposed to believe that something is a virtue only if it is; and assuming we can know what is *not* a virtue, the same must go for that. For Unqualified Constructivism, that I am disposed to believe that *a*, *b*, *c* are virtues entails that they are. For Externalism, that this disposition is a method by which I form beliefs about virtue entails that it is reliable. I need not be infallible, but for the most part, what I am disposed to believe is true. It follows in turn, on either view, that we are disposed to converge in our beliefs, that we are disposed to agree (or not to disagree) on what the virtues are. And this, I submit, is not the case. As I argued at the beginning of chapter one, it is possible to disagree about reason and virtue in ways that

---

[68] Boyd 1988; Brink 2001.
[69] Jackson 1998: Chs. 5–6.

are both pervasive and fundamental. One's views about how to live may be dramatically false. That is the position of those who believe that selfishness or 'enlightened self-interest' is the only ethical virtue. Their beliefs are radically unreliable; they do not converge with mine.

It might be argued, in response, that the implications of accuracy and agreement here are weak. What follows from the views above is only that we are *disposed* to believe the truth. We may not actually believe it. As a general matter, dispositions can be 'masked'.[70] From the fact that a glass is disposed to break when struck, it does not follow that it will do so inevitably; the manifestation of this disposition may be prevented by external circumstance, as when the glass is stuffed with packing materials. Likewise, we may be disposed to believe ethical propositions only when they are true, and yet have false beliefs. We do not manifest every tendency we possess. The problem is that even in this modest form, the doctrine of convergence or reliability fails. Not everyone who has the concept of virtue is disposed to apply it accurately, so that the only cause of error is the kind of interference in which a disposition is masked. It is at least possible, and arguably not uncommon, to be brought up so as to lack this disposition altogether. We cannot dismiss this possibility by pretending that corruption always masks a persisting disposition to get things right. For a disposition cannot be masked by an entrenched property of its own possessor. If my nature is such that I reliably do not ϕ in C, I am not disposed to ϕ in C.[71]

---

[70] The term is due to Mark Johnston (1992: 233); the phenomenon of masking is further discussed in Bird 1998 and Fara 2005.

[71] The prospect of 'intrinsic masking' is quite generally controversial: see Choi 2005 for an argument against, and Clarke 2010 for a response. Clarke notes a defect in Choi's principal argument (Clarke 2010: 157) and gives plausible examples of transient masking of one disposition by another, as when I am disposed to fall asleep when tired but do not do so because I tend to stay awake when I take caffeine. The possibility of entrenched or stable masking, even by extrinsic factors, has also

In striving to resist such doubts, Wedgwood places on the normativity of the intentional more weight than it is able to bear. Even if it is true that in order to possess a concept or attitude one must be disposed to conform to a corresponding principle of reason,[72] these principles may be minimal: standards of logic or coherence, not ideal rationality. This distinction makes room for a modest version of charity: in interpreting someone correctly, we aim for 'a theory that finds him consistent, a believer of [empirical] truths' but not necessarily 'a lover of the good'.[73] There is no hidden contradiction in the idea of someone whose beliefs about virtue are reliably and systematically false. As David Lewis argued in a similar context, we cannot extract even approximate convergence in values from the nature of ethical thought.[74]

This, then, is our predicament. If ethical knowledge is possible, some of us must be reliable in our beliefs, and our reliability cannot be an accident. In particular, it must be explained, in part, by the constitutive connection of attitude and ethical fact. But the explanation cannot imply that we are *all* disposed to get things right. It must leave room for those who are by nature unreliable. Putting things in the first person: if I have ethical knowledge and you do not, there must be an explanation of my reliability that does not entail yours. Short of a bizarre metaphysics on which the facts are constitutively tied to my beliefs but not to those of other people, what could the explanation be?

---

been denied: see Fara 2005: 76–8, and Clarke 2010: 157–8 for another response. Clarke's examples here are less compelling. A glass under permanent protection may still be fragile, as he insists, but is it disposed to break when struck? The principle in the text is in any case weaker: that there is no possibility of entrenched, intrinsic masking. As far as I know, there is no serious challenge to this claim.

[72] Wedgwood 2007: 168–9.

[73] The quoted words appear in Davidson 1970: 222, though without the contrast I propose. In later work, Davidson applies the more ambitious line—on which we must be 'lovers of the good'—to the objectivity of value; see Davidson 1995: 49–51.

[74] Lewis 1989: 134–5; see also McDowell 1986: 379 on 'the local character of any ethical convergences . . . it is sensible to expect'.

We can bring out the depth of the problem here by working through some constructivist moves. A first thought is that we have assumed a version of constructivism on which it follows that a, b, c are virtues from the fact that I am disposed to think they are. What if we insist on unanimity? Something is a virtue only if the disposition to think that it is a virtue is common to those who share the relevant concept. It is thus quite possible for me to go badly wrong. The defects of this view are obvious. If unanimity is required, the possibility of divergence in belief will mean that there are no ethical virtues. A single stubborn egoist eliminates most, holding that self-interest is the only virtue. The selfless altruist eliminates even that. As we saw in chapter one, philosophical disagreement about practical reason is no less extreme. At the same time, unanimous constructivism frustrates the attempt to satisfy K. We can no longer give a constitutive explanation on which the reliability of my methods follows from the fact that I use them, since my methods or dispositions may not be shared. This problem is solved by a relativistic view on which the virtues 'for me' are bound to my dispositions, while the virtues 'for you' are bound to yours. The truth-conditions of 'a is a virtue' vary from speaker to speaker and turn on what they are disposed to think. Again, the defect is obvious. This account destroys or limits the scope for interpersonal disagreement: when our dispositions vary widely, we are talking past each other, and our claims can be both be true. But this is not the case.[75]

At this point, the solution may seem clear. What makes convergence look incredible is a focus on unqualified dispositions. If you ask what we are disposed to believe about virtue, but place no conditions on how we are brought up, or how our beliefs are formed, you cannot expect much common ground. Most

---

[75] Here I reject 'contextualism' or 'speaker relativism' in ethics. As noted in the introduction, some 'relativists' allow for cognitive disputes, even between members of different communities; their views are not at issue here.

constructivists hold more subtle views. They appeal to what we are disposed to think if we are non-ethically well-informed, under conditions of ideal reflection or critical scrutiny, from an impartial perspective or behind a veil of ignorance. We can represent such views, schematically, as follows:

QUALIFIED CONSTRUCTIVISM: For a trait to be a virtue is for us to be disposed to think that it is a virtue in condition C.

If this is our conception of virtue, we predict convergence only when condition C is realized and the relevant dispositions are unmasked. If C is sufficiently robust, this prediction may be true.[76] The question is whether it makes room for ethical knowledge. The answer may seem to be yes. If Qualified Constructivism holds, and I am disposed to form beliefs about virtue in condition C, it follows from the nature of virtue that I am sufficiently reliable. In that sense, the truth of my beliefs is not an accident. But this is not enough to satisfy K. The problem is that, for all we have said so far, my tendency to form beliefs in C, instead of some other condition, may be unrelated to the fact that beliefs formed in C are true. In terms of K: we don't get a constitutive explanation on which it follows from the fact that I use m—the method of forming beliefs in condition C—that m is reliable, as we did with Unqualified Constructivism. The most we get is that if I use m, I am using a reliable method. Its being reliable and my using it are unconnected with one another.

The upshot is that, where unqualified constructivists face the dilemma of implausible convergence or relativity, the qualified constructivist avoids these threats at the cost of ethical knowledge. It is not enough that beliefs formed in C are made reliable by the nature of virtue, if it is still an accident that I use a reliable method in forming my beliefs. What the qualified constructivist needs is a connection between my use of a method and its being reliable,

---

[76] For doubts about achieving this non-trivially, see Wright 1988: §§IV–V.

a demand that takes us back to externalist themes. We saw above that Externalism is consistent with both reductive and non-reductive metaphysics; it is also consistent with Qualified Constructivism. If part of what it is to have the concept of ethical virtue is to be such that one's method for identifying traits as virtues is sufficiently reliable, and the most reliable method is to form beliefs in C, it follows that those who have the concept of virtue are disposed to form beliefs in something like condition C, and that their reliability is no accident. An account of this kind satisfies K, and so makes sense of ethical knowledge, on externalist grounds. It is Externalism, not constructivism, that does the crucial work.

The downside is that we are back to convergence or relativity. If those who have the concept of virtue are bound to be reliable, and they are concerned with the same range of facts, they will tend to agree (or not to disagree) about what they are. In avoiding this result, there is a final strategy to consider. In section 2, we faced a challenge to a priori knowledge quite similar to the one we are confronting here. Such knowledge could be explained if part of what it is to possess a concept is that one's non-evidential methods be sufficiently reliable. The difficulty is that concept-possession is social, and that it is possible to grasp a concept through one's conceptual or linguistic community while being mostly wrong in the groundless beliefs in which that concept figures. The solution was to find reliability at the social level, and to argue that K is satisfied when the relevant social fact explains the individual's method. We can make the same move here, shifting from individual externalism to something like this:

Social Externalism: Part of what it is to have the concept of ethical virtue is to belong to a conceptual or linguistic community whose method for identifying traits as virtues is sufficiently reliable.

Suppose that S uses m to identify traits as virtues, and he uses m because the community does. That the community uses m is a generic claim, consistent with exceptions, not a universal general-ization. It follows from this claim, together with Social External-ism, that m is reliable. This story is sufficient to satisfy K. We have an explanation of why S uses m that entails its reliability through the nature of the facts involved. At the same time, we allow for individuals who have the concept of virtue but lack any disposition to believe the truth.

Once we see the possibility of Social Externalism, we can antici-pate, too, a social interpretation of constructivism: for a trait to be a virtue is for the members of one's conceptual or linguistic community to believe that it is a virtue. If I am disposed to think that certain traits are virtues because my community does, it follows by Social Constructivism that my method is reliable, and the condition in K is met. But not everyone is so disposed.

This is, I think, the best one can do with the resources imagined thus far. It is not enough. While social versions of externalism and constructivism leave room for unreliable subjects, they do not allow for whole communities to go astray. But this, too, is possible. In the wrong conditions, a society of human beings might be quite generally disposed to false beliefs about virtue, even when they are non-ethically well-informed.[77] Think of the community of rational egoists in chapter one. This problem would be solved by social relativism, on which the truth-conditions of virtue-claims vary between societies, turning on the methods they are disposed to use. The community of egoists may be reliable about virtue 'for them' but not 'for us'. (This prospect is close to the surface in Social Constructivism.) Although it saves the explanation of reliability, however, this picture conflicts with a guiding assump-tion of this book: that, exceptions aside, when we seem to disagree in ethics, we do. The clash between a community of altruists and

[77] In my view, this marks a contrast between ethical and epistemic facts. Epis-temological disagreement is impossible between communities that are non-epistemically well-informed. Social externalism may thus explain our knowledge of epistemology.

one of egoists is a cognitive dispute. They do not talk past each other, but make conflicting claims about virtue, which cannot all be true.

Unlike the possibility of unreliable individuals, the possibility of unreliable communities might be questioned or denied. Perhaps a society in such pervasive error could not exist, or would lack the concept of virtue. I do not know how to prove otherwise, though I am sure it is not the case. Human nature is sufficiently plastic that a whole community could be corrupt: not disposed to believe the truth in a way that could explain the reliability of individuals and thereby satisfy K.[78] None of the accounts we have seen is able to accommodate this. We have found no explanation of reliability, and thus of ethical knowledge, on which a community can be disposed to get things wrong. Depressing though it is, we must accept this possibility. But then the challenge is profound. Without the help of social convergence, can ethical knowledge be saved?

[78] On the anthropological evidence for this claim, see the final section of chapter four.

4

Human Nature

The problem of ethical knowledge turns on the tension between two things: the need to explain our reliability so that the truth of our beliefs can be no accident, and the need to leave room for communities that are not at all reliable. The first constraint cannot be met unless the facts are constitutively bound to us. But in the obvious forms of externalism and constructivism, constitutive connections yield predictions of reliability, at least at the social level, that fail the second constraint. It is this constraint that distinguishes knowledge in ethics from a priori knowledge, as such. Elsewhere, the implications of Social Externalism for convergence in belief are sound. In many cases, it is impossible for the linguistic or conceptual community that originates a concept to be unreliable in their groundless beliefs about its application. When an individual's methods are explained by the methods of this community, her reliability is no accident. Not so for the concepts of right and wrong, or of what there is reason to do.

We are left with a quandary. Is there any way to escape the dilemma of convergence and relativity, to explain the reliability of some communities and individuals, without predicting reliability for all? In section I of this concluding chapter, I argue that there is. We can allow for ethical knowledge without God by making explanatory use of human nature. This approach will place demands on the natural history of human life, and on its metaphysics, that some may find implausible. Roughly put, the claim is that human beings are, by nature, disposed to believe the truth. Though it allows for societies that lack this disposition, and so does not imply social convergence, this claim might still be false. In section 2, I ask whether we can live without it. The argument of the previous chapter was concerned exclusively with knowledge, not with justified belief. Can we give up on one but save the other? We might concede that ethical knowledge is impossible, so long as we are justified in believing what we do. Against this concessive view, I hold that we do have ethical knowledge, and that we need it, or its possibility in principle, for justified belief. In the final section, I turn to the metaphysics and anthropology of human nature, arguing that the claims required for ethical knowledge are not incredible. We cannot live without knowledge in ethics, but we can hope for the knowledge we need.

1. KNOWLEDGE WITHOUT CONVERGENCE

Although I have argued against it, Social Externalism is right about one thing. If we hope to make sense of non-accidental reliability without convergence or relativity, we must look to general facts that explain why individuals are reliable while leaving room for those who are not. For social externalists, the relevant facts concern the methods of a conceptual or linguistic community. These facts are generic, not universal: that the community uses m is consistent with exceptions, subjects who use some other method, m', which may not be reliable at all. What we need are generalizations of this kind, only ones that permit a whole community to go astray. We need something that transcends communities but can explain how individuals go on.

In what follows, I explore the prospect of an explanatory turn to human nature or the 'life form' of our species. I do so with caution. Like the theories of inductive and a priori knowledge in chapter three, the theses offered here will be schematic. We are not in a position to state the details. Nor am I sure that a theory on these lines is actually true; that issue will be saved for section 3. What I argue is that we can make sense of ethical knowledge, without social convergence, only if the facts are bound to us through human nature. If we know right from wrong, it is generalities about the life form of the human being that connect us to ethical facts.[1]

My inspiration here is a revived Aristotelianism about living things that finds its fullest expression in Michael Thompson's essay, 'The Representation of Life'.[2] Thompson contends that there are forms of generality that permit exceptions even as they state the nature or essence of what they generalize about. Such generality is common in natural history. Thompson writes:

Let us call the thoughts expressed in the field guide and in the nature documentary *natural-historical judgments*. We may take as their canonical expression sentences of the form 'The S is (or has, or does) F'—'The domestic cat has four legs, two eyes, two ears, and guts in its belly'; 'The Texas bluebonnet harbors nitrogen-fixing microbes in certain nodes on its roots'; 'The yellow finch breeds in spring, attracting its mate with such and such song'; whatever. [Such] *sentences* I will call 'Aristotelian categoricals'. Our language of course permits the same judgments to be expressed in a number of ways, for example, by 'S's are/have/do F' or 'It belongs to an S to be/have/do F' or 'S's characteristically (or typically) are/have/do F' or 'This is (part of) how S's live: they are/have/do F', and a hundred others. (Thompson 2008: 64–5)

Like the descriptions of a community that figured in social versions of externalism and constructivism, the sentences mentioned here are generic, not universal. Not all generics aim to specify a form of life or the nature of a kind, but some do, and their doing so does not require exceptionless generality. That wolves hunt in

---

[1] To repeat the proviso above: this claim ignores the appeal to God in moral epistemology.

[2] Reprinted with revisions as Part One of *Life and Action* (Thompson 2008). Thompson is drawing on brief remarks by Anscombe (1958: 38); see also Moravcsik 1994.

packs is some sort of insight into what they are, even if this one or that one may go it alone. Likewise, the fact that human beings have thirty-two teeth.

Thompson goes on to make extraordinary claims about the propositions of natural history. He believes that they display a form of judgement, a kind of generality or nexus of subject and predicate, unique to living things. The difference between life form generalizations and other generic propositions is as deep as the contrast between universal and existential quantification, and like that contrast, belongs to the form and not the content of thought. It is in this sense that *life* is a logical category: to be alive is to fall under a concept that is itself the subject of natural-historical truths.[3] These claims are hard to believe. Is there really a difference of *form* between natural-historical judgements and generic propositions of other kinds? I am sceptical about this view, and nothing I say below depends on it. Nor does it matter for our discussion whether natural history is irreducible, as Thompson's work suggests, or whether it can be explained in other terms. I will make no assumptions about that, drawing instead on our untutored grasp of what is said by Thompson's botanist or student of zoology. What matters now is that their generalizations are true, and that they are neither statistical or universal, not that they are logically or metaphysically primitive. It also matters that natural-historical facts can be explanatory. At least on occasion, the fact that the S is by nature F explains why this particular S is F.[4] Its being F is not an accident. I have two arms, two eyes, and the capacity for articulate speech because I am a human being, and human beings have these things. That this proposition makes sense, and that it is true, can be acknowledged by everyone, whatever its truth involves.[5]

---

[3] Thompson 2008: 76–82.

[4] On the sort of explanation involved here, see Thompson 2008: 202–7.

[5] We come back to this question, though briefly, in section 3.

As well as being independent of Thompson's wilder claims, appeal to natural history as the source of ethical knowledge does not imply the Aristotelian ethics of Philippa Foot.[6] Nor is Foot's doctrine of 'natural goodness' enough to satisfy K. According to Foot, human virtue consists in the natural goodness of the human will, where the standard of natural goodness is supplied by natural history. Roughly speaking:

NATURAL VIRTUE: For a trait to be a human virtue is for human beings to act in accordance with that trait.[7]

In interpreting Natural Virtue, we should bear in mind that 'Human beings act justly' is a natural-historical judgement consistent with even a majority of exceptions. As Thompson notes, 'although "the mayfly" breeds shortly before dying, *most* mayflies die long before breeding' (Thompson 2008: 68). Still, if human beings by nature act justly, that can explain why S acts justly, and so how it is no accident that S is just. What it cannot explain is the possibility of ethical knowledge. Taken by itself, Natural Virtue does not provide a constitutive explanation of reliability because it does not connect fact with belief.[8] What we need is a relation between the two that runs through human nature, a form of externalism or constructivism that shifts from communities to forms of life:

NATURAL EXTERNALISM: Part of what it is to have the concept of ethical virtue is to belong to a life form whose method for identifying traits as virtues is sufficiently reliable.[9]

---

[6] Foot 2001.

[7] Here I apply the 'simple-minded principle of inference' for natural defect offered by Thompson (2008: 80) to the standard of human virtue. Foot's actual view is more complex, but not in ways that matter to our discussion.

[8] This is the application to Natural Virtue of a point about Reductionism in the previous chapter, near the beginning of section 3.

[9] Alternatively: that I have acquired the concept from such a life form, to allow for aliens whose grasp of ethical concepts is parasitic on ours.

NATURAL CONSTRUCTIVISM: For a trait to be a virtue is for creatures of one's life form to believe that it is a virtue.

For natural externalists, the reference of ethical concepts is mediated not by conceptual or linguistic community, but by human nature itself. Our ethical concepts refer to properties tracked by the methods human beings by nature employ. For natural constructivists, ethical facts are fixed by the ethical beliefs of human beings, not those of the individual or his society. On either view, a human being, S, may be disposed to believe that a, b, c are virtues because human beings are so disposed, an explanation that entails her reliability through the nature of the facts involved. For Natural Externalism, the entailment runs through the nature of ethical belief. For Natural Constructivism, it runs through the nature of ethical virtue. It does not follow from this that I have ethical knowledge only if my method is infallible. The degree of reliability in one's method required for knowledge was left open in chapter three, but it must fall short of perfection. Thus, if human beings use m, it follows by Natural Externalism that m is sufficiently reliable; and if I use m', which is similar to m, because human beings use m, that is enough to satisfy K.

Foot's theory can thus be transposed from Natural Virtue to claims about ethical fact and belief that explain the possibility of ethical knowledge. What does the epistemic work in these accounts is not the idea of human nature as, directly, a standard of virtue, but as having the power to connect our attitudes with the facts in a way that allows for individuals, and even whole communities, to go astray. We may doubt that, as a matter of natural history, the human being is perfectly virtuous—just, benevolent, courageous—as Foot's theory appears to predict.[10]

---

[10] Assuming a principle endorsed by Thompson (2008: 69) that 'The S is F' and 'The S is G' together entail 'The S is both F and G'. As Thompson notes, this pattern may be repeated endlessly so as to produce 'a true statement of our form involving a complex conjunctive predicate that is not true of *any* member of the kind denoted by its subject, living or dead. I mean: nobody's perfect' (Thompson 2008: 72).

How human beings by nature live is not the measure of how they should. But epistemically speaking, that doesn't matter. What we need is Natural Externalism or Natural Constructivism, not Natural Virtue. On either view, it is not an accident when a human being comes to be reliable about virtue in the course of natural development—though natural development may be rare. Ethical knowledge may not be historically prevalent; but it is not impossible.

What happens to the dilemma of convergence and relativity when we turn to human nature as the foundation of ethics? We no longer need Social Externalism or Social Constructivism; there is no risk of social relativism. Whole communities may be disposed to false beliefs about human virtue, a common subject matter on which we disagree. That human beings by nature value justice or benevolence is consistent with societies that do not. We do, however, embrace a kind of relativism. Imagine a life form different from ours, but able to reason practically, to act intentionally, and to engage in what looks like ethical thought. For simplicity, we can suppose that they speak a language homophonic with English, guiding their lives by what they call 'virtues'. But their method for identifying 'virtues' is not like ours and their beliefs are shocking. Perhaps they are led to regard self-interest as the only 'virtue'. According to Natural Externalism and Natural Constructivism, 'virtue' is not virtue. The aliens do not have ethical concepts and do not contradict us when they say 'Self-interest is the only virtue.' Instead, we are talking past each other. We might have hoped that ethics would speak in the same voice to all rational beings. Not so on the present approach.

How bad is this result? Not, I think, as bad as it may seem. There are frames of mind in which life-form-relativity makes sense. If our natural history were quite different, if we reproduced asexually or lived for millions of years, if we were non-social animals or rational wolves, we might have different ethical concepts, ones with which we could correctly say 'Justice is not a virtue.'[11] Having recognized this, we could introduce an explicitly relativized concept, *virtue-for-kind-K*.[12] In these terms, we can say that human-virtues might differ from alien. Once we are used to these ideas, we can extend them to less dramatic variations in natural history. Nor should we assume that it is possible for living things to be exactly like us, except in their ethical concepts. For it to belong to the natural history of a form of life that they approve of cruelty and call it 'virtue', doing so must play a coherent role in how they survive and flourish; their natural history would have to be different from ours in many other ways.

Still, some philosophers will resist. The concepts of practical reason, they will urge, cannot be in this way relative: they must be shared by rational beings, as such. Such resistance prompts a question with which I close. If we need a connection between fact and belief in ethics that transcends communities, why stop at human nature and so invite the charge of relativism? Why not advert to rational nature itself? On this alternative, a trait is a virtue just in case rational beings believe that it is a virtue, or it belongs to the concept of ethical virtue that rational beings are reliable in using it. Again, the generality involved is non-universal. That rational beings by nature value justice or benevolence is meant to be consistent with individuals, communities, and even rational life forms, that do not.

The problem is that not every kind supports such generalizations.[13] When Fs are by nature G, in the generic sense, though some Fs are not G, that a particular F is G depends on the

---

[11] On rational wolves, see McDowell 1995a: §3. McDowell invents the wolves in objecting to a certain kind of ethical naturalism, for which he cites Foot. But the objection turns on treating appeal to the needs of the wolf as giving a *reason* to be virtuous, whereas for Foot, and for us, its role is metaphysical. Facts about the nature of a kind explain the possibility of ethical knowledge; as McDowell insists, 'we should not try to picture [them] as what directly engages the will of a [virtuous] person' (McDowell 1995a: 191).

[12] This kind of relativity is explicit in the work of Thompson and Foot.

[13] The reflections that follow are adapted from Setiya 2010a: §4.

circumstance in which it finds itself. The conditions required for an F to become G, and in which such development fails, themselves belong to the natural history of the F. They specify the needs that must be met, the internal conditions, and the proper environment, in which an F is G. Thompson illustrates this point with an example:

Now suppose I say, 'Bobcats breed in spring': it is again obvious that this isn't going to happen in any particular case unless certain conditions are satisfied. Perhaps a special hormone must be released in late winter. And perhaps the hormone will not be released if the bobcat is too close to sea level, or if it fails to pass through the shade of a certain sort of tall pine. But, now, to articulate *these* conditions is to advance one's teaching about bobcats. It is not a reflection on the limited significance of one's original teaching. The thought that *certain hormones are released*, or that *they live at such and such altitudes and amid such and such vegetation*, is a thought of the same kind as the thought that *they breed in spring*. The field guide and the nature documentary assign an external environment to the intended life-form, after all, and in the same mood or voice or discursive form they elsewhere employ in describing its bearers' inner structure and operations. These conditions are thus 'presupposed' by the life-form itself; and how the bearer comes to arrive at them will itself be described in natural-historical terms. (Thompson 2008: 71)

This applies to generalizations about human nature. It is only when our needs are met and our environment suitable that we fully manifest what we are. Thus, if humans beings believe that justice is a virtue, or use a method that vindicates that claim, still some do not—as, perhaps, when they are brought up in conditions of neglect or hunger or abuse. That these conditions prevent the realization of human nature is part of our natural history.[14] Our proper environment is one that fosters the tendency to value justice. Or if it is not, then human beings do not by nature value justice, after all. The central point is this: when Fs are by nature G,

[14] On the objectivity of human needs, and their place in our form of life, see Foot 2001: 41–3.

but some Fs are not G, there are further truths about the nature of the F that describe its development, environment, and needs; when an F fails to be G, these truths should tell us why.[15] With this in mind, what to make of the claim that rational beings regard justice as a virtue, or use a method that generates that belief, though some individuals, communities, and rational life forms do not? For this to be the case, there must be truths about the nature of rational beings, as such, that explain how they come to value justice, and describe the conditions in which such development fails. But this requirement makes no sense. There is no such thing as the natural environment of a rational being, abstractly conceived, as there is for particular kinds of living thing. In short, the rational being is not characterized by a *system* of natural-historical truths that speak to development, environment, and need; but natural-historical claims—as, for instance, that human beings value justice—cannot stand alone.

It follows that we cannot capture the nature of rational beings in merely generic terms. If it belongs to rational beings, as such, to believe that justice is a virtue, or to use a method that vindicates that claim, this fact implies a universal generalization. All rational beings share that belief, or use that method. This argument explains why the turn to generics is a turn away from rational nature as the explanatory ground of ethical knowledge towards natural history or the human life form. If we hope to make room for individuals and communities that are not disposed to believe the truth in ethics, and yet to satisfy K, the relativity of virtue is the cost. Our ethical concepts turn on the natural history of human life; they would not be shared by rational wolves.

---

[15] It does not follow that a normal F is G, only that the conditions of failure belong to natural history. Thus, birds by nature lay eggs, though normal males do not. The point is that the natural history of birds gives the conditions under which they lay eggs, including the division of the sexes. The relationship between generics and what is normal for a kind is explored by Nickel 2009, who cites the existing literature.

If this is right, we can know objective ethical facts—facts that are not socially relative—only if those facts are bound to us through human nature. If ethical concepts are not life-form-relative, ethical facts cannot be known. Those who recoil from relativism, even in this moderate form, may be tempted to accept this consequence. How bad would it be, they might ask, if ethical knowledge were impossible? Maybe not so bad, if we have justified beliefs. In the following section, I address this view, defending the existence of, and the need for, ethical knowledge.

2. JUSTIFICATION

Suppose you are adamant that ethics is not relative to form of life and that it is therefore impossible to satisfy K. Can you simply admit that there is a problem of ethical knowledge, concede its sceptical result, and persist in your beliefs? These beliefs, you maintain, are epistemically justified, though we cannot know that they are true. For all that has been said, this strategy is viable even if ethical facts are wholly irreducible and independent of us. Is the argument of chapter three too narrow to generate sceptical doubt?

The first thing to say about this response is that its concession is too great. It is shocking to be told that we do not know that torture is wrong, that there is reason to care for others, that it is unjust to treat whole populations as slaves. We do know these things and we need to explain how. What is perhaps worse, once we conclude that we do not know that p, there is pressure to admit that it might not be the case. Torture might be permissible, there may be no reason to care for anyone but oneself, slavery might be morally just. None of these claims is true.

The second thing to say about abandoning ethical knowledge is that it is not clear we can do so without losing justified belief. In order to show this, we need to appeal to a principle that connects the two. For instance, it might be thought that one cannot be justified in believing p if one knows that one does not know it. But this is not exactly right. When I enter a lottery, I do not know that my ticket will lose and I know that I do not know it. At the same time, I am justified in being extremely confident that I will not win. Those who hope for justified belief in ethics, but are willing to sacrifice knowledge, may be satisfied with this. Closer to the mark is the principle that one cannot be justified in believing p if knowledge about its topic is impossible. If the obstacles to knowledge are not local but systematic—if there is, as a matter of necessity, no way to know how things stand in a certain domain—it is epistemically out of reach. It cannot be the object of justified belief. The challenge for this suggestion is to individuate topics in such a way as to make it plausible. Is there something incoherent in the view that we cannot know the future, but that predictions are warranted? Is the future a topic of its own, or does it consist of familiar topics viewed in a distinctive way? These questions are hard to address. And they seem irrelevant. What matters is not the object of knowledge, but its source or mode. On a more illuminating view, the connection between justified belief and knowledge is that when a belief is justified, it is the perhaps imperfect manifestation of a capacity to know. If someone is justified in believing p, we can always ask *how*. The answer specifies a capacity for knowledge: inductive, perceptual, whatever. In each case, there is an account of the capacity on which it can deliver knowledge, in accordance with K. In the particular case, it may have failed to do so: one's belief is merely justified, and potentially false. Such failures may be widespread. But there are conditions in which the capacity works: it issues in knowledge of the relevant kind.[16]

[16] Because it ties justification to knowledge only in one condition—that in which one's reliability would be no accident—this principle allows for justified beliefs in wildly deceptive worlds. For this demand as a problem for reliabilism and for the relationship of justification and truth, see Cohen 1984.

If this is right, we cannot have justified ethical beliefs unless they are traced to a capacity to know. In a certain range of cases, this capacity might be testimonial. We can know things by being told. But this merely defers the question. According to the argument of this book, we cannot have knowledge in ethics unless the facts are constitutively bound to us. If we have the capacity to know what we ought to do, or how we ought to be, that is because our method is explained by the life form of the human being, where it is a condition of having ethical concepts that one belong to a life form whose method is reliable. Or it is because our beliefs are explained by human nature, where generalities about the beliefs of human beings constitute ethical facts.

How do these views make sense of justified belief? The issue is easier to discuss in the case of Natural Externalism. (It can be adapted to Natural Constructivism if we replace the simple formulation for belief with one in which ethical facts are constituted by the verdicts of our ethical methods.) Assuming a Reductive Epistemology, the proper method in ethics is to go from evidence that x is N to the belief that x is E, where necessarily, if x is N then x is E. Suppose I use this method, or something close to it, because human beings do. It follows by Natural Externalism that my method is reliable, so that K is satisfied. I can know right from wrong, virtue from vice. But there is room for justification without knowledge. I might have strong evidence that x is N even though it is not, and conclude on the basis of this evidence that x is E, a belief that is justified but false. In a Gettier case, my belief could be justified and true, yet not amount to knowledge, as when my evidence that x is N is accurate by chance.[17] At the same time, if I lacked the capacity for knowledge altogether, if I were not disposed to use a method that is more or less reliable, or my reliability were accidental, it would not be a source

[17] Gettier 1963.

of justification. Unless my method is explained by human nature, ethical knowledge is impossible—as is justified belief.

Why accept the crucial premise of this argument, that justified belief involves the exercise of a capacity to know? The short answer is that we need to relate knowledge to justification somehow or other: these are not two independent standards, but aspects of a unified domain. Nor is it enough to say that knowledge entails justification, leaving the implication unexplained. If knowledge were justified true belief, there would be no mystery here. But the lesson of Gettier is that it is not. We might add further conditions. Maybe knowledge is justified true belief that satisfies K. But there are bound to be exceptions. And we in any case lose the desired unity. On this conception, knowledge is the product of two standards, justification and K, neither of which is grounded in the other. The same point holds for other accounts of knowledge that supplement truth, justification, and belief. In contrast, if justified belief is the perhaps imperfect manifestation of a capacity to know, the relationship of justification to knowledge is both unified and relatively clear.

There is more to say about this line of thought, which raises broader questions in epistemology. It seems to me to capture the legitimate core of McDowell's complaint, in 'Knowledge and the Internal', about the status of 'hybrid' views. Such views purport to build knowledge from conditions distinct from justification (a standing in the space of reasons) together with justified belief.[18] Unlike McDowell, however, we need not regard the epistemic position of those with justified false beliefs as worse than that of those with knowledge, except in the trivial sense that they fail to know. Nor does it follow from the argument above that grounds for knowledge are invariably factive, as McDowell claims. We

---

[18] McDowell 1995b: 402–4.

can know on the basis of defeasible evidence.[19] The point is that, in doing so, we display a capacity for knowledge that is exercised, imperfectly, even in justified false belief.

Despite its modesty, this principle might be denied; I cannot argue for it adequately here. Whatever its fate, the basic fact survives: that it is bad enough to admit that we do not know the injustice of torture or slavery, that we have mere justification for these claims. To repeat: according to the argument of this book, such knowledge is possible only if human beings accept the injustice of torture and slavery, or use a method that generates those beliefs. The question that remains is whether this condition is met. Does human nature sustain the truths in ethics we aspire to know?

3. FAITH

In section 1, we saw that the appeal to human nature as the ground of ethical knowledge could take substantially different forms:

NATURAL EXTERNALISM: Part of what it is to have the concept of ethical virtue is to belong to a life form whose method for identifying traits as virtues is sufficiently reliable.

NATURAL CONSTRUCTIVISM: For a trait to be a virtue is for creatures of one's life form to believe that it is a virtue.

In each case, the facts about our life form that make ethical knowledge possible are generalizations that permit exceptions. They exploit the generality that figures in the nature documentary, in the natural history of a life form, in this case *us*. In my view, the

[19] As is clear from inductive, as opposed to perceptual knowledge. McDowell comes close to seeing this (at McDowell 1995b: 410–12), but his response is puzzling. He argues that perceptual knowledge would be impossible without theoretical knowledge of the world. But this is at most a response to complete inductive scepticism. It does not show how to construct each item of inductive knowledge on factive grounds.

most plausible connection here takes the shape of Natural Externalism, on which the reference of ethical concepts turns on the method of ethical inquiry characteristic of human life. This theory is, I believe, in the spirit of David Hume, whose criterion of virtue in the sentiments produced by sympathy from the 'general point of view' has no deeper foundation than the practice of using ethical language to track these sentiments, a practice he takes to be shared by humankind.[20]

Unlike Natural Constructivism, Natural Externalism is only apparently circular. Where natural constructivists explain what it is for something to be an ethical virtue in terms of beliefs about virtue, natural externalists could state their view as follows: part of what it is to have the concept of ethical virtue is to belong to a life form whose method for applying that concept is sufficiently reliable.[21] This is at most a partial account of ethical concepts, the part that is most relevant to epistemology. A full development would explain the role of such concepts in guiding action, such as it is, and their relation to our sentiments. Both empirical work and a priori judgement suggest that possession of ethical concepts rests in some way on emotional or affective response.[22] Here, too, I am inclined to agree with Hume. The path from ethical concepts to their referents is mediated not only by nature but by feeling. But the intricacies are hard to work out. We can speak to the nature of ethical concepts, I believe, only in a general way, arguing for connections of one shape of another. We are not in a position to resolve the details. Although I will speculate about the way our concepts work, below, our epistemic infirmity will be a persistent theme.

From now on, I focus on what is common to externalism and constructivism in their natural-historical forms. How do these

---

[20] Hume *Treatise*, Book Three.

[21] Or to have acquired it from a life form of this kind.

[22] On the empirical evidence, see Prinz 2007: Ch. 1, though he overstates the case in identifying sentiments with moral concepts, and emotions with judgements. McDowell 1985 and Wiggins 1987 give a priori grounds for sentimentalism.

views make sense of ethical knowledge? They do so by allowing explanations of our methods or beliefs in terms of human nature, explanations that entail their reliability through the nature of ethical concepts or ethical facts. The crucial implication shared by these accounts is that human beings are by nature reliable in ethics; their beliefs tend to be true, their methods reflect the facts. Again, this is a natural-historical claim, consistent with exceptions. It does not follow that every human being, or every human society, is disposed to get things right. Nor does it follow that human beings act in accordance with their ethical beliefs. It is an advantage of Natural Externalism and Natural Constructivism over Natural Virtue that they are modest about this. If justice and benevolence are virtues, human beings are disposed to think they are, or to use a method that generates that belief; they may not be just and benevolent in what they do. It is easier to hope that human beings by nature recognize the virtues than that they act in accordance with them. Whether we can sustain this hope is the question with which we will end.

Before we get to that, a brief digression into metaphysics. Natural Constructivism is a reductionist theory. If it is true, we can say what it is for a trait to be a virtue using non-ethical concepts: concepts of human nature and belief. Natural Externalism is not itself reductionist, but it makes room for Reductionism. If ethical concepts denote the properties tracked by the method of inquiry characteristic of human life, they denote properties for which Reductionism may hold. Our method for identifying traits as virtues may track a property whose nature can be described in social-psychological terms. To be a virtue is to have this property. If there are general problems for Reductionism, they apply to these claims. Think of the open question argument: when I concede that x is N, I can still ask whether x is E.[23] Does it follow that being N is not the same as being E? For familiar reasons, it does not. When

---

[23] Moore 1903: Ch. 1.

being F is the same as being G, it need not be obvious or analytic that all Fs are G. The most we can conclude is that the concept, *being F*, is not the concept, *being G*.

A more ambitious use of Moore is sometimes made.[24] According to this argument, the proposition that all Fs are G can be informative, when being F is being G, only if the concepts, *being F* and *being G* pick out a single property in different ways. It is informative to learn that water is H_2O because the concept H_2O picks out this kind by its chemical nature, while the concept *water* picks it out as the stuff that quenches thirst, falls from the clouds as rain, and so on. The informational content of the identity claim is captured by those other concepts. This picture leads to a dilemma. If being E is being N, how does the concept *being E* pick out the property in question, so that it is informative to learn that what is N is E? Could it do so in non-ethical terms? No, since the concept *being E* would then be equivalent to a non-ethical concept, and Moore's open question would close. On the other hand, if *being E* picks out its referent by another ethical concept, *being F*, which explains how the identity is informative, we are no further on. Reductionism must apply to the property of being F, and the same dilemma applies. Barring circularity or regress, we must eventually resort to the first response, explaining an ethical concept in non-ethical terms. If Moore is right that the question 'It is N, but is it E?' is always open, Reductionism fails.

What should we make of this argument? Its mistake is to assume that, when it is informative to learn that being N is being E, the content of *being E* can be analysed in other terms. The reductionist should deny this premise. The concepts *being N* and *being E* pick out a single property in different ways, but the mode of presentation involved in *being E* need not rely on other concepts. If this mode of presentation is non-descriptive but distinct from

---

[24] See Bilgrami 2004: §III; Parfit 2011: §§93–5.

the mode of presentation involved in *being N*, the identity can be informative while avoiding the dilemma above.

Though there is more to say about the general issue of Reductionism, we will not pursue it here. Instead, we turn to what is distinctive of the present approach: its appeal to human nature or natural history, to the claim that we are by nature reliable in ethics, even though some, perhaps many, are deceived. Begin with a radical objection: that we cannot speak of human nature at all. In an influential 1986 address, David Hull complained that species cannot be defined by common properties; variation is part of the natural order. Given the extent of variation among the members of our species, we cannot expect to discover a meaningful essence that could count as human nature. What Hull rejects in making this argument is, however, quite different from what we need. He is concerned with essence or nature as an explanatory specification of necessary and sufficient conditions, on the model of water as H_2O. We are concerned with generalizations about a life form that admit exceptions, sometimes many of them, and which explain the properties of individuals. The facts of variation do not preclude the existence of law-like generalizations that play this role.[25] Nor do they enforce a merely statistical reading. One of Thompson's insights in 'The Representation of Life' is that, taken at face value, the generalizations of natural history obey a principle of conjunction: 'The S is F' and 'The S is G' together entail 'The S is both F and G'. This rules out a statistical interpretation.[26] It is generalizations of this non-universal, non-statistical kind that appear in the nature documentary, and in the specification of human nature that matters to us. The critic of human nature must deny that the claims of the nature documentary make sense, or that they can be true—or show that no such documentary could be made about human life. We have seen no case for this.

[25] For different versions of this point, see Dupré 2002: 155–6; Machery 2008.
[26] Thompson 2008: 69, 72.

Hull's arguments raise a larger issue, which can only be touched on here: the relationship between forms of life described in nat-ural-historical terms and conceptions of species in biology. In identifying species, biologists appeal to such conflicting criteria as typology, morphology, reproductive isolation, evolution, and genetics. It is not clear which of these are relevant to the identity of life forms. Nor does identity of species, understood in any of these ways, appear sufficient for identity in form of life. In criticiz-ing ethical appeals to human nature, Philip Kitcher presents the following case:

Consider a possible world in which the history of life on earth is very much like ours up to the point at which the speciation event that gave rise to our species occurred. In the first generation of the species that become reproductively isolated from the ancestral hominids, there were two sorts of genotypes, both of which are present in actual human populations. One of these sorts of genotypes includes many combinations of alleles that we would count as normal . . . , the other includes combinations of alleles that cause a disruption of normal metabolism, allowing amino acids to build up in the body with profound neurological conse-quences . . . Unfortunately, the ancestral environment contains plants that are toxic to anyone with the normal genotype. . . . Thus, in the first generation, all the normals die, without any of them ever developing to the stage at which they could have rich mental lives. The abnormal genotype confers protection against the toxin. . . . Hence, in the entire history of the species, no individual ever develops a rich mental life. (Kitcher 1999: 72)

Kitcher's point is that higher mental functioning is not essential to *homo sapiens*. His thought experiment could be run for other properties, too. Its most salient consequence, from our point of view, is that our life form is contingent, relative to our member-ship in the biological species. Kitcher's scenario is one in which the natural history of *homo sapiens* differs from ours. The anthropolo-gist in this possible world should tell a different story from that of actual anthropologists. If we individuate life forms by natural history, as we have been doing, Kitcher is describing a different form of life.[27]

Our question, then, is what the anthropologist should say about us as we actually are. If ethical knowledge is explained by human nature, human beings are disposed to believe the truth as a matter of natural-historical fact. Assuming, as I do, that justice and benevolence are virtues, that we should care about the rights and needs of others, these are propositions about which humans beings by nature agree. Could that be true? Is it rational to suppose that human beings are by nature reliable in ethics? Is this a form of wishful thinking refuted by the facts?

In addressing this question, it is important not to overstate the implication of reliability in Natural Externalism. What the principle claims is that our method of identifying traits as virtues is sufficiently reliable. The method need not be as simple as believing certain truths. As we saw in section 2, and earlier in chapter one, the method of Reductive Epistemology goes from evidence that x is N to the belief that x is E, where necessarily, if x is N then x is E. For this method to give the right output it needs the right input: reliable evidence of the facts on which the truth in ethics supervenes. It is enough to sustain the prospect of non-accidental truth that we tend to get things right in those conditions. In the version stated above, Natural Constructivism appeals directly to our beliefs. But it can be revised on similar lines: for a trait to be a virtue is for it to be identified as such by the methods characteristic of human beings, methods that Reductive Epistemology may describe. The upshot is a qualified doctrine of reliability: human beings are disposed to believe the truth in ethics in conditions of non-ethical information. Though it is weaker than

[27] This verdict prompts perplexing questions about the metaphysics of natural history and the historicity of human nature. We will return to them, briefly, at the end.

the claim of true belief, this prediction is optimistic. Can it be maintained?

The empirical study of ethical belief is in its infancy; but we can make a start. Questions about the place of ethics in human nature have become entangled, in recent work, with the issue of 'nativism': whether ethical judgement and its content are innate. In this context, innate capacities are both evolved and dedicated or domain-specific.[28] According to Marc Hauser, 'we are equipped with a moral faculty—an organ of the mind that carries a universal grammar of action' (Hauser 2006: 11). This grammar places constraints on the range of possible variation in ethical systems. Others have complained that, while we are biologically prone to certain values, ethics is not innate but a byproduct of cognitive powers that evolved for other reasons.[29] Whatever the interest of this dispute, it is not directly relevant to us. That it belongs to our natural history to engage in ethical thought, and to reach particular views, is consistent with the absence of an ethical faculty. Nor does it matter, for our purposes, whether ethical judgement and its content are side effects of other cognitive gains, or whether they were selected for. We are in the orbit of anthropology, not evolution or cognitive science.

In an essay on the state of the field, Jonathan Haidt and Craig Joseph report that

in all human cultures, individuals react with flashes of feeling linked to moral intuitions when they perceive certain events in their social worlds: when they see others (particularly young others) suffering, and others causing that suffering; when they see others cheat or fail to repay favors; and when they see others who are disrespectful or who do not behave in a manner befitting their status in the group. (Haidt and Joseph 2004: 58)[30]

---

[28] See Prinz 2008: 370.
[29] Prinz 2007: Ch. 7, 2008.
[30] See also Hauser 2006: 48.

They go on to offer an explanation of these facts in terms of innate functioning. We are interested in the description itself. There seem to be cross-cultural norms governing harm and suffering, fairness and reciprocity, hierarchy and respect. In virtually every human culture, harm is taken to be prima facie wrong, and so to stand in need of justification. Fair distribution is approved, free-riding criticized. Parents and authorities are thought to deserve respect, at least when they do their part.

Are there cultures that lack these attitudes altogether? Maybe so. According to a well-known ethnography, the Ik of northern Uganda engage in constant deception, steal food from their elders by force, and take pleasure in the suffering of children.[31] But such cases have little significance. That human beings believe in the virtues of justice, benevolence, and respect is consistent with particular societies that do not.[32] What is more, we can often explain why their circumstance should be anomalous or not conducive to the expression of human nature. The culture of the Ik is in part of the product of generations of starvation and drought, the enduring deprivation of basic human needs.[33]

Even if we share some abstract values, the question remains how far their content is culturally fixed. Is there evidence of profound, pervasive, and widespread disagreement about the standards of justice, or benevolence, or respect? This is one of the points, predicted above, at which we must acknowledge how little we know. Among the examples of ethical diversity most commonly cited in recent work are Aztec cannibalism, sharp contrasts in the norms that apply to marriage, incest, and the family, and conflicting attitudes to violence in the American North

[31] Turnbull 1972. This account has been disputed in subsequent work; for references, see Moody-Adams 1997: 79–80.

[32] For a similar response, see Hauser 2006: 166.

[33] The same point applies, in a weaker form, to the Inuit and Yanomamö, other cultures said to have disturbing attitudes to killing and violence. On the relevance of needs to the natural history of a life form, see the end of section 1.

and South.[34] Each of these examples is problematic. In the case of marriage and the family, there may be a range of attitudes consistent with human nature. While some arrangements are unjust, others vary in permissible ways. Human beings by nature accept a variety of marital and familial structures. The differences between them are matters of cultural convention not ethical fact. A more general point is that, according to the qualified doctrine of natural reliability, what matters to the prospect of ethical knowledge is truth in conditions of non-ethical information. That human beings are reliable in this circumstance is consistent with dramatic error in the presence of false beliefs. This fact casts doubt on the case of Aztec cannibalism, bound up as it is with a false cosmology. (It does not matter whether this cosmology developed post hoc; the question is whether belief in the permissibility of cannibalism would survive without it.) In a trenchant discussion of cultural relativism, Jesse Prinz contends that nothing like this could explain the difference in attitudes to violence in America.[35] Men in the American South are much more prone to think violence permissible in response to infidelity and to public expressions of disrespect.[36] But the contrast is far from clear. Different attitudes to violence could be explained by different 'situational meanings': different perceptions of what happens when one is insulted, different expectations about the perceptions of others. The meaning of an action is context-sensitive.[37] Thus, if you had a vivid sense of the contempt that others would feel for you if you ignored an insult, and you would feel it yourself, that might affect your ethical beliefs. What is more, for someone to treat you in this way,

---

[34] See, for instance, Prinz 2007: Ch. 5.

[35] Prinz 2007: 193–4; see also Doris and Plakias 2008: 316–22.

[36] Nisbett and Cohen 1996.

[37] On situational meaning, see Moody-Adams 1997: 34–7, and on the danger of projecting descriptions of action from one cultural context to another, Cook 1999: Chs. 7–12.

knowing these facts, is for them to do something that would not be possible if the facts did not obtain.[38]

Some of the most difficult questions here concern the *scope* of justice, benevolence, and respect. Do human beings by nature apply these virtues and their demands to the treatment of every human being, at least when they know the facts outside of ethics itself? If not, are they sufficiently reliable? The topic is elusive and hard to resolve. But there is evidence that the systematic exclusion of others from the scope of ethical treatment turns on a denial of their humanity. In *Less Than Human*, David Livingstone Smith explores the role of 'dehumanization' in slavery, genocide, and war.[39] He argues persuasively that the moral disengagement that makes genocide possible turns on a failure to recognize the common humanity of oneself and another. Human beings do not find it permissible to engage in the mass killing of their fellows. Rather, because they believe this would be wrong, they are able to accept genocide only by denying or refusing to acknowledge the humanity of those who are killed. They conceive their victims as vermin or as predators, creatures that seem human but in fact belong to another natural kind. Smith's book gives graphic and disturbing evidence of the extent to which such thinking is pervasive in the history of genocide and how seriously it is taken by those who participate in it.[40]

Likewise, if we look at the history of slavery, we find belief in its justice bound up, at different times, with different false beliefs. The history of American slavery is in part a history of biological or metaphysical racism, the view that races are subspecies of

---

[38] Nisbett and Cohen themselves cite the different expectations of Southerners faced with threats or insults: knowing the risk of violence from others can explain a pre-emptively violent response; see Nisbett and Cohen 1996: 38.

[39] Smith 2011: Chs. 3–5.

[40] This history is independent of his more speculative claims about the evolved psychology of dehumanization; compare Smith 2011: Chs. 6–8.

humanity, some inferior to others.[41] Before such conceptions emerged in the eighteenth century, and for some time afterwards, the defence of slavery involved mistakes not about race but about the heritability and permanence of cultural and religious differences, about the content of revealed religion, and about divine hierarchy as a ground of unequal treatment that could answer the charge of ethical arbitrariness or luck.[42] Ancient Greek and Roman slavery did not involve beliefs of this kind: its ethical arbitrariness was apparent to those who practised it. With the notorious exception of Aristotle, ancient Greeks did not believe that being a slave was a natural identity but a matter of contingent misfortune.[43] It is not clear, however, that they regarded slavery as just. Presumably, there were sufficient doubts to prompt Aristotle's account of natural slavery in the *Politics*. And for many, the question of justice and injustice did not arise: it must be permissible to keep slaves since slaves were essential to communal life, which was ethically required.[44] It takes a work of imagination to see the feasibility of radically different social arrangements. (As Bernard Williams cautions in his treatment of these issues, we must be open to the possibility that our own conceptions of justice rest on similar mistakes.)[45]

---

[41] On the history of slavery in general, see Davis 1966; Meltzer 1993. For a brief account of American racism, its evolution, and its role in slavery, and a comparison with European anti-Semitism, see Frederickson 2002. The ideologies of European colonialism and of American segregation were also explicitly racist.

[42] Again, see Frederickson 2002: Ch. 1; and on religion and slavery, Davis 1966: Chs. 4 and 6; Meltzer 1993, Vol. 1: 5–6, 205–7, 211–12, 223–4; Garnsey 1996.

[43] For a philosophically sensitive discussion of slavery in the ancient world, see Williams 1993: Ch. V; and for a partly conflicting view, Isaac 2004: Ch. 2. If Isaac is right about the emergence of racism in Greek and Roman culture, that would only strengthen the connection of moral error to false belief.

[44] Williams 1993: 112–13, 116–17. On slavery as a 'necessary evil' in Enlightenment thought, see Davis 1966: Chs. 13–14.

[45] Williams 1993: 124–5. Does the argument of this paragraph imply that slavery would be just if the relevant beliefs were true? For two reasons, no. First, even if it is not the case that human beings judge slavery unjust when they have certain beliefs, it does not follow that they hold it to be just when they believe those things. (After all, we are not so disposed.) Second, it is consistent with our reliability that we go

Though we have only scratched the surface, none of the cases considered so far, and none of the cases I have found in the literature on cultural relativism, refutes the doctrine of natural reliability: that human beings are reliable in ethics when their beliefs are non-ethically well-informed.[46] Understood in this way, natural reliability is consistent with actual disagreement, even of pervasive kinds. And it tolerates exceptions. In adverse conditions, a whole society might go astray. Think of the community of rational egoists imagined in chapter one. Not impossible, I believe, but not how human beings by nature turn out.[47]

In chapter three, I argued against Externalism and Constructivism about virtue on the ground that they predict an implausible convergence in ethical belief. These views entail the reliability of anyone who can think about virtue at all. The implication of Social Externalism and Social Constructivism is more modest: that any community with the concept of virtue is disposed to get things right. That a community is reliable is a generic claim, consistent with exceptions: individuals whose beliefs are well-informed but

wrong about slavery in this particular case, so long as we do not go so badly wrong as to find it permissible in fact.

[46] A more complete account would go piecemeal through the anthropological treatments. I cannot do that here; the task has been pursued by others. See especially Moody-Adams 1997: Chs. 1–2 and Cook 1999: Chs. 7–14 on Benedict 1934 and Herskovits 1964, 1972. It must also address the history of women's oppression and subordination by men. Materials for an account on which belief in the justice of patriarchy involves mistakes about the nature of women, about divine hierarchy, and about social possibility, can be assembled from the classic history by Gerda Lerner; see, especially, Lerner 1986: Ch. 11, 1993: 3–4, and on women's right to education, Ch. 9.

[47] This prompts a revised account of ethical disagreement. In the earlier treatment, I said that we should not defer to moral monsters—the community of rational egoists—however coherent and numerous they are. Suppose, however, that there is nothing unnatural in their acculturation or environment. Their existence would then conflict with the claims about human nature implied by our ethical beliefs. If we recognize these facts, our beliefs will be cast in doubt. It matters that the conditions required for this—the existence of a community with whom we are in radical disagreement, but whose development cannot be faulted on other grounds—have not in fact been met.

wildly false. But it is still too strong. Hence the turn to natural history. That human beings are by nature reliable would follow from the general reliability of individuals or societies that engage in ethical thought. But it is logically weaker. Unlike social versions of externalism and constructivism, the doctrine of natural reliability allows for unreliable communities. It is the minimal prediction of convergence in ethics sufficient for ethical knowledge.

In the last few pages, I have urged that this prediction may be true. Only 'may be' in that the empirical evidence is sparse. This evidence does not upset the claim that, in conditions of natural development and non-ethical information, human beings are reliable in ethics: they value justice, benevolence, and respect, along with such virtues as courage, temperance, and adequate self-regard, conceiving these virtues in roughly the same way. But it does not support this, either. Since human beings have existed almost always in conditions of dramatic ignorance and reflective failure, deprivation and imperfect development, empirical predictions of convergence in such conditions are speculative to a high degree. We are left with a final, difficult question: what attitude should we take to ethics in this epistemic predicament? What is it rational to believe about the prospect of ethical knowledge?

The first thing to say is that, while the empirical evidence is hard to gauge, it indicates that the facts in ethics may be less determinate than some of us suppose. It is one thing to say that human beings by nature value justice, benevolence, and the rest, and that they conceive these virtues in roughly the same way. It is another thing to say that human beings agree on the intricate details, that quite specific conceptions of justice and so on are fixed by human nature. With hesitation, then, I accept the contention of Haidt and Joseph that cross-cultural virtues take culturally determined forms.[48] The germ of wisdom in cultural relativism is that we should be cautious in condemning alien practices that may turn

---

[48] Haidt and Joseph 2004; see also Hauser 2006: 43–4, 82–4, 299–300.

out, in the end, to be permissible variations on values we share. About the extent of this variation, we are—so far as the empirical evidence goes—pretty much in the dark.

There is a further reason for modesty. In light of K and the turn to natural history, to claim that one knows an ethical fact is to claim that one's method is explained by human nature. It is because human beings form ethical beliefs by a method that vindicates one's claim that one believes what one does. This may be true for belief in the virtues listed above. It is unlikely to be true across the board. Much of what we believe in ethics, we do not know. To echo Mill in *The Subjection of Women*:[49] there is no reason to suppose that the present state of humankind is the perfect expression of human nature, that there is no room for us to become more fully what we are.

This modesty may suggest a yet more radical thought: not that human nature is historically unrealized, but that once we sever it from the essence of the species, it is not historically fixed. The questions raised by this proposal are, for me, among the most disorienting in philosophy. Can human nature change over centuries or millennia? The true anthropology of the present might then differ from the anthropology of a thousand years ago.[50] Or should the anthropologist's narrative itself be historical, describing phases in the organized development of a life form?[51] I do not think we are in a position to say. Our ignorance is not

[49] Mill 1869: Ch. I.

[50] This argument is endorsed by John Dupré: 'Being highly—indeed in important respects uniquely—social creatures it is not surprising that the developmental cycles by which we are reproduced contain massive inputs of a social character. Presumably, it is the malleability of this contribution . . . that accounts for the speed at which human nature changes over historical time. And of course, given this conception, it is a very important possibility that there may be intentional input into these changes such that human nature may perhaps, in the long run, be a product of human creation' (Dupré 2002: 165–6). On the relative contributions of genes and culture to human behaviour, see Ehrlich 2000; Boyd and Richerson 2005.

[51] As in historical materialism.

just empirical: it turns on the primitive state of philosophical anthropology. It is partly for this reason that I have not tried to formulate a detailed view about the content of ethical thought, or its precise relationship with human nature. Nor have I gone far into the metaphysics of natural history. What I have argued is more abstract: that ethical knowledge is possible, without God, only if the facts are bound to us by aspects of our nature that can explain how beliefs are formed.

Confronted with so much doubt, so many questions, one could be forgiven for grasping at the other way out. If God deliberately gives us, or some of us, reliable dispositions, our reliability will be no accident even if the facts about which we are reliable are irreducible and constitutively independent of us. It is a thesis of this book that knowledge of absolute ethical facts, whose concepts are not life-form-relative, is possible only if God or something similar—the Form of the Good, perhaps—plays this explanatory role.

I cannot believe it, myself. Nor do I think we should fear the prospect of life-form-relativity, or despair of human nature. In *Finite and Infinite Goods*, Robert Adams writes that 'faith is, or involves, believing something that a rational person might be seriously tempted to doubt, or not to believe' (Adams 1999: 373–4). It is also a kind of 'pro-attitude': to have faith in something is to be *for* it, not against it.[52] Adams thinks of moral belief, in general, as a matter of faith.[53] If I am right about the conditions of ethical knowledge, to believe that they are met is to have a certain faith in human nature. Thinking that justice and benevolence are human virtues, and that I know they are, I infer that human beings agree with me, at least in the right conditions. In that sense, human nature is fundamentally good. The inference is risky, its

---

[52] Adams 1999: 384.
[53] Adams 1999: 374–5.

conclusion one that a reasonable person might doubt or deny. Although I accept it, I cannot prove that it is true. At the same time, faith in humanity does not conflict with what is empirically known. It is not irrational to hope. In the absence of God, I do not see how else we can defend our ethical beliefs.

BIBLIOGRAPHY

Adams, R. 1999. *Finite and Infinite Goods*. Oxford: Oxford University Press.

Anscombe, G. E. M. 1958. Modern moral philosophy. Reprinted in *Ethics, Religion and Politics*. Oxford: Blackwell, 1981: 26–42.

Audi, R. 2004. *The Good in the Right*. Princeton, NJ: Princeton University Press.

Bealer, G. 1999. A theory of the a priori. *Philosophical Perspectives* 13: 29–55.

Bedau, M. 1991. Can biological teleology be naturalized? *Journal of Philosophy* 88: 647–55.

Bedke, M. 2010. Developmental process reliabilism. *Erkenntnis* 73: 1–17.

Benacerraf, P. 1973. Mathematical truth. *Journal of Philosophy* 70: 661–79.

Benedict, R. 1934. *Patterns of Culture*. Boston, MA: Houghton Mifflin.

Bigelow, J. and Pargetter, R. 1987. Functions. *Journal of Philosophy* 84: 181–96.

Bilgrami, A. 2004. Intentionality and norms. In M. De Caro and D. Macarthur, eds., *Naturalism in Question*. Cambridge, MA: Harvard University Press, 2004: 125–51.

Bird, A. 1998. Dispositions and antidotes. *Philosophical Quarterly* 48: 227–34.

——2003. Nozick's fourth condition. *Facta Philosophica* 5: 141–51.

Blackburn, S. 1993. *Essays in Quasi-Realism*. Oxford: Oxford University Press.

——1998. *Ruling Passions*. Oxford: Oxford University Press.

Boghossian, P. 1996. Analyticity reconsidered. *Noûs* 33: 360–91.

——2003. Blind reasoning. *Proceedings of the Aristotelian Society, Supplementary Volume* 77: 225–48.

Boyd, R. 1988. How to be a moral realist. In G. Sayre-McCord, ed., *Essays on Moral Realism*. Ithaca, NY: Cornell University Press, 1988: 181–228.

——and Richerson, P. 2005. *The Origin and Evolution of Cultures*. Oxford: Oxford University Press.

Briggs, R. 2009. Distorted reflection. *Philosophical Review* 118: 59–85.

Brink, D. 1989. *Moral Realism and the Foundations of Ethics*. Cambridge: Cambridge University Press.

——2001. Realism, naturalism, and moral semantics. *Social Philosophy and Policy* 18: 154–76.

Broome, J. 1997. Reasons and motivation. *Proceedings of the Aristotelian Society, Supplementary Volume* 71: 131–46.

Burge, T. 1979. Individualism and the mental. *Midwest Studies in Philosophy* 4: 73–121.

——1986. Intellectual norms and foundations of mind. *Journal of Philosophy* 83: 697–720.

——2003. Perceptual entitlement. *Philosophy and Phenomenological Research* 67: 503–48.

Burgess, J. and Rosen, G. 1997. *A Subject with No Object*. Oxford: Oxford University Press.

Choi, S. 2005. Do categorical ascriptions entail counterfactual conditionals? *Philosophical Quarterly* 55: 495–503.

Christensen, D. 2007. Epistemology of disagreement: the good news. *Philosophical Review* 116: 187–217.

Clarke, R. 2010. Opposing powers. *Philosophical Studies* 149: 153–60.

Cohen, S. 1984. Justification and truth. *Philosophical Studies* 46: 279–95.

——1999. Contextualism, skepticism, and the structure of reasons. *Philosophical Perspectives* 13: 57–89.

——2010. Bootstrapping, defeasible reasoning, and *a priori* justification. *Philosophical Perspectives* 24: 141–59.

Cook, J. W. 1999. *Morality and Cultural Differences*. Oxford: Oxford University Press.

Dancy, J. 2010. Moral perception. *Proceedings of the Aristotelian Society, Supplementary Volume* 84: 99–117.

Daniels, N. 1979. Wide reflective equilibrium and theory acceptance in ethics. *Journal of Philosophy* 76: 256–82.

Davidson, D. 1970. Mental events. Reprinted in *Essays on Actions and Events*. Oxford: Oxford University Press, 1980: 207–25.

——1983. A coherence theory of truth and knowledge. Reprinted in *Subjective, Intersubjective, Objective*. Oxford: Oxford University Press, 2001: 137–53.

——1995. The objectivity of values. Reprinted in *Problems of Rationality*. Oxford: Oxford University Press, 2004: 39–51.

Davis, D. B. 1966. *The Problem of Slavery in Western Culture*. Ithaca, NY: Cornell University Press.

Doris, J. and Plakias, A. 2008. How to argue about disagreement: evaluative diversity and moral realism. In W. Sinnott-Armstrong, ed., *Moral Psychology, Volume 2*. Cambridge, MA: MIT Press, 2008: 303–31.

Dreier, J. 1997. Humean doubts about the practical justification of morality. In G. Cullity and B. Gaut, eds., *Ethics and Practical Reason*. Oxford: Oxford University Press, 1997: 81–100.

Driver, J. 2006. Autonomy and the asymmetry problem for moral expertise. *Philosophical Studies* 128: 619–44.

Dummett, M. 1973. *Frege: Philosophy of Language*. London: Duckworth.

Dupré, J. 2002. Darwin and human nature. In *Humans and Other Animals*. Oxford: Oxford University Press, 2002: 151–71.

Dworkin, R. 1996. Objectivity and truth: you'd better believe it. *Philosophy and Public Affairs* 25: 87–139.

Ehrlich, P. R. 2000. *Human Natures: Genes, Cultures, and the Human Prospect*. London: Penguin.

Elga, A. 2007. Reflection and disagreement. *Noûs* 41: 478–502.

Enoch, D. 2010. The epistemological challenge to metanormative realism. *Philosophical Studies* 148: 413–38.

Fara, M. 2005. Dispositions and habituals. *Noûs* 38: 43–82.

Feldman, R. 1985. Reliability and justification. *The Monist* 68: 159–74.

——2006. Epistemological puzzles about disagreement. In S. Hetherington, ed., *Epistemology Futures*. Oxford: Oxford University Press, 2006: 216–36.

Field, H. 1989. *Realism, Mathematics and Modality*. Oxford: Blackwell.

Fine, K. 1994. Essence and modality. *Philosophical Perspectives* 8: 1–16.

——2001. The question of realism. *Philosophers' Imprint* 1: 1–30.

Foot, P. 1958. Moral arguments. Reprinted in *Virtues and Vices*; second edition. Oxford: Oxford University Press, 2002: 96–109.

——1958-9. Moral beliefs. Reprinted in *Virtues and Vices*; second edition. Oxford: Oxford University Press, 2002: 110–31.

——2001. *Natural Goodness*. Oxford: Oxford University Press.

——2002. *Virtues and Vices*; second edition. Oxford: Oxford University Press.

Frederickson, G. M. 2002. *Racism: A Short History*. Princeton, NJ: Princeton University Press.

Garnsey, P. 1996. *Ideas of Slavery from Aristotle to Augustine*. Cambridge: Cambridge University Press.

Gauthier, D. 1986. *Morals by Agreement*. Oxford: Oxford University Press.

Gettier, E. 1963. Is justified true belief knowledge? *Analysis* 96: 121–3.

Gibbard, A. 1990. *Wise Choices, Apt Feelings*. Cambridge, MA: Harvard University Press.

——2003. *Thinking How to Live*. Cambridge, MA: Harvard University Press.

Godfrey-Smith, P. 1994. A modern history theory of functions. *Noûs* 28: 344–62.

Goldman, A. 1986. *Epistemology and Cognition*. Cambridge, MA: Harvard University Press.

Haidt, J. and Joseph, C. 2004. Intuitive ethics: how innately prepared intuitions generate culturally variable virtues. *Daedalus* 133: 55–66.

Hampton, J. 1998. *The Authority of Reason*. Cambridge: Cambridge University Press.

Harman, G. 1973. *Thought*. Princeton, NJ: Princeton University Press.

——1977. *The Nature of Morality*. Oxford: Oxford University Press.

——1986. *Change in View*. Cambridge, MA: MIT Press.

Hauser, M. 2006. *Moral Minds*. New York, NY: Harper Collins.

Hawthorne, J. 2002. Deeply contingent a priori knowledge. *Philosophy and Phenomenological Research* 65: 247–69.

Herskovits, M. 1964. *Man and His Works*. New York, NY: Knopf.

——1972. *Cultural Relativism*. New York, NY: Random House.

Hills, A. 2009. Moral testimony and moral epistemology. *Ethics* 120: 94–127.

Hobbes, T. 1651. *Leviathan*, edited by E. Curley. Indianapolis, IN: Hackett Publishing, 1994.

Hopkins, R. 2007. What is wrong with moral testimony? *Philosophy and Phenomenological Research* 74: 611–34.

Horwich, P. 2005. Meaning constitution and epistemic rationality. In *Reflections on Meaning*. Oxford: Oxford University Press, 2005: 134–73.

Hubin, D. C. 1999. What's special about Humeanism? *Noûs* 33: 30–45.

——2001. The groundless normativity of instrumental reason. *Journal of Philosophy* 98: 445–68.

Hull, D. 1986. On human nature. *Proceedings of the Biennial Meeting of the Philosophy of Science Association* 2: 3–13.

Hume, D. 1739–40. *A Treatise of Human Nature*, edited by D. F. Norton and M. Norton. Oxford: Oxford University Press, 2007.

——1748. *An Enquiry Concerning Human Understanding*, edited by T. Beauchamp. Oxford: Oxford University Press, 2000.

Hursthouse, R. 2006. Practical wisdom: a mundane account. *Proceedings of the Aristotelian Society* 106: 285–309.

Isaac, B. 2004. *The Invention of Racism in Classical Antiquity.* Princeton, NJ: Princeton University Press.

Jackson, F. 1998. *From Metaphysics to Ethics.* Oxford: Oxford University Press.

Johnston, M. 1992. How to speak of the colors. *Philosophical Studies* 68: 221–63.

——2001. The authority of affect. *Philosophy and Phenomenological Research* 63: 181–214.

Jones, K. 1999. Second-hand moral knowledge. *Journal of Philosophy* 96: 55–78.

Joyce, R. 2006. *The Evolution of Morality.* Cambridge, MA: MIT Press.

Kagan, S. 1989. *The Limits of Morality.* Oxford: Oxford University Press.

——2001. Thinking about cases. *Social Philosophy and Policy* 18: 44–63.

Kahane, G. 2011. Evolutionary debunking arguments. *Noûs* 45: 103–25.

Kelly, T. 2005. The epistemic significance of disagreement. *Oxford Studies in Epistemology* 1: 167–96.

——2010. Peer disagreement and higher-order evidence. In R. Feldman and T. Warfield, eds., *Disagreement.* Oxford: Oxford University Press, 2010: 111–74.

Kitcher, P. 1999. Essence and perfection. *Ethics* 110: 59–83.

Klein, P. 1981. *Certainty: A Refutation of Scepticism.* Minneapolis, MN: University of Minnesota Press.

Korsgaard, C. 2003. Realism and constructivism in twentieth-century moral philosophy. Reprinted in *The Constitution of Agency.* Oxford: Oxford University Press, 2008: 302–26.

Kripke, S. 1980. *Naming and Necessity.* Cambridge, MA: Harvard University Press.

——2011. Nozick on knowledge. In *Philosophical Troubles.* Oxford: Oxford University Press, 2011: 162–224.

Lerner, G. 1986. *The Creation of Patriarchy.* Oxford: Oxford University Press.

——1993. *The Creation of Feminist Consciousness.* Oxford: Oxford University Press.

Lewis, D. 1989. Dispositional theories of value. *Proceedings of the Aristotelian Society, Supplementary Volume* 63: 113–38.

MacFarlane, J. 2005. Making sense of relative truth. *Proceedings of the Aristotelian Society* 105: 321–39.

——2007. Relativism and disagreement. *Philosophical Studies* 132: 17–31.

Machery, E. 2008. A plea for human nature. *Philosophical Psychology* 21: 321–9.

Mackie, J. L. 1977. *Ethics: Inventing Right and Wrong.* Harmondsworth: Penguin.

Majors, B. and Sawyer, S. 2005. The epistemological argument for content externalism. *Philosophical Perspectives* 19: 257–80.

Manning, R. N. 1997. Biological function, selection, and reduction. *British Journal for the Philosophy of Science* 48: 69–82.

Matthen, M. 1999. Evolution, Wisconsin style: selection and the explanation of individual traits. *British Journal for the Philosophy of Science* 50: 143–50.

McDowell, J. 1985. Values and secondary qualities. Reprinted in *Mind, Value, and Reality.* Cambridge, MA: Harvard University Press, 1998: 131–50.

——1986. Critical notice of Bernard Williams, *Ethics and the Limits of Philosophy. Mind* 95: 377–86.

——1994. *Mind and World.* Cambridge, MA: Harvard University Press.

——1995a. Two sorts of naturalism. Reprinted in *Mind, Value, and Reality.* Cambridge, MA: Harvard University Press, 1998: 167–97.

——1995b. Knowledge and the internal. Reprinted in *Meaning, Knowledge, and Reality.* Cambridge, MA: Harvard University Press, 1998: 395–413.

——1998. *Mind, Value, and Reality.* Cambridge, MA: Harvard University Press.

——2008. The disjunctive conception of experience as material for a transcendental argument. Reprinted in *The Engaged Intellect.* Cambridge, MA: Harvard University Press, 2009: 225–40.

McGrath, S. 2004. Moral knowledge by perception. *Philosophical Perspectives* 18: 209–28.

——2008. Moral disagreement and moral expertise. *Oxford Studies in Metaethics* 3: 87–107.

——2009. The puzzle of pure moral deference. *Philosophical Perspectives* 23: 321–44.

——2011. Skepticism about moral expertise as a puzzle for moral realism. *Journal of Philosophy* 108: 111–37.

Meltzer, M. 1993. *Slavery: A World History.* New York, NY: Da Capo Press.

Mill, J. S. 1869. *The Subjection of Women*, edited by S. M. Okin. Indianapolis, IN: Hackett Publishing, 1988.

Miller, R. 1985. Ways of moral learning. *Philosophical Review* 94: 507–56.

Millikan, R. G. 1984. Naturalist reflections on knowledge. *Pacific Philosophical Quarterly* 65: 315–34.

——1989. In defense of proper functions. *Philosophy of Science* 56: 288–302.

Moody-Adams, M. 1997. *Fieldwork in Familiar Places*. Cambridge, MA: Harvard University Press.

Moore, G. E. 1903. *Principia Ethica*. Cambridge: Cambridge University Press.

Moravcsik, J. 1994. Essences, powers and generic propositions. In T. Scaltsas, D. Charles, and M. L. Gill, eds., *Unity, Identity and Explanation in Aristotle's Metaphysics*. Oxford: Oxford University Press, 1994: 229–44.

Nagel, T. 1970. *The Possibility of Altruism*. Princeton, NJ: Princeton University Press.

——1986. *The View from Nowhere*. Oxford: Oxford University Press.

Neander, K. 1991. The teleological notion of 'function'. *Australasian Journal of Philosophy* 69: 454–68.

Neta, R. and Rohrbaugh, G. 2004. Luminosity and the safety of knowledge. *Pacific Philosophical Quarterly* 85: 396–406.

Nickel, B. 2009. Generics and the ways of normality. *Linguistics and Philosophy* 31: 629–48.

Nickel, P. 2001. Moral testimony and its authority. *Ethical Theory and Moral Practice* 4: 253–66.

Nisbett, R. E. and Cohen, D. 1996. *Culture of Honor: The Psychology of Violence in the South*. Boulder, CO: Westview Press.

Nozick, R. 1981. *Philosophical Explanations*. Cambridge, MA: Harvard University Press.

Oddie, G. 2005. *Value, Reality, and Desire*. Oxford: Oxford University Press.

Owen, D. 1999. *Hume's Reason*. Oxford: Oxford University Press.

Parfit, D. 1997. Reasons and motivation. *Proceedings of the Aristotelian Society, Supplementary Volume* 71: 99–130.

——2006. Normativity. *Oxford Studies in Metaethics* 1: 325–80.

——2011. *On What Matters*. Oxford: Oxford University Press.

Peacocke, C. 1993. How are a priori truths possible? *European Journal of Philosophy* 1: 175–99.

——2004. *The Realm of Reason*. Oxford: Oxford University Press.

Plantinga, A. 1993a. *Warrant: The Current Debate*. Oxford: Oxford University Press.

——1993b. *Warrant and Proper Function*. Oxford: Oxford University Press.

Prinz, J. 2007. *The Emotional Construction of Morals*. Oxford: Oxford University Press.

——2008. Is morality innate? In W. Sinnott-Armstrong, ed., *Moral Psychology, Volume 1*. Cambridge, MA: MIT Press, 2008: 367–406.

Pritchard, D. 2005. *Epistemic Luck*. Oxford: Oxford University Press.

Pryor, J. 2000. The skeptic and the dogmatist. *Noûs* 34: 517–49.

——2004. What's wrong with Moore's argument? *Philosophical Issues* 14: 349–78.

Quine, W. V. 1969. Natural kinds. In *Ontological Relativity and Other Essays*. New York, NY: Columbia University Press, 1969: 114–38.

Rawls, J. 1951. Outline of a decision procedure for ethics. *Philosophical Review* 60: 177–97.

——1970. *A Theory of Justice*. Cambridge, MA: Harvard University Press.

——1975. The independence of moral theory. *Proceedings and Addresses of the American Philosophical Association* 48: 5–22.

Richard, M. 2008. *When Truth Gives Out*. Oxford: Oxford University Press.

Ross, W. D. 1930. *The Right and the Good*. Oxford: Oxford University Press.

Sainsbury, M. 1997. Easy possibilities. *Philosophy and Phenomenological Research* 57: 907–19.

Sayre-McCord, G. 1996. Coherentist epistemology and moral theory. In W. Sinnott-Armstrong and M. Timmons, eds., *Moral Knowledge?* Oxford: Oxford University Press, 1996: 137–89.

Scanlon, T. M. 1998. *What We Owe to Each Other*. Cambridge, MA: Harvard University Press.

——2002. Rawls on justification. In S. Freeman, ed., *Cambridge Companion to Rawls*. Cambridge: Cambridge University Press, 2002: 139–67.

Schafer, K. 2010. Evolution and normative skepticism. *Australasian Journal of Philosophy* 88: 471–88.

Schiffer, S. 2004. Skepticism and the vagaries of justified belief. *Philosophical Studies* 119: 161–84.

Setiya, K. 2007. *Reasons without Rationalism*. Princeton, NJ: Princeton University Press.

——2010a. Sympathy for the devil. In S. Tenenbaum, ed., *Desire, Practical Reason, and the Good*. Oxford: Oxford University Press, 2010: 82–110.

——2010b. Does moral theory corrupt youth? *Philosophical Topics* 38: 205–22.

Shafer-Landau, R. 2003. *Moral Realism: A Defence*. Oxford: Oxford University Press.

Shaver, R. 1999. *Rational Egoism: A Selective and Critical History.* Cambridge: Cambridge University Press.

Sidgwick, H. 1907. *The Methods of Ethics*; seventh edition. London: Macmillan.

Silins, N. forthcoming. Explaining perceptual entitlement. *Erkenntnis.*

Sinnott-Armstrong, W. 2002. Moral relativity and intuitionism. *Philosophical Issues* 12: 305–28.

Smith, D. L. 2011. *Less Than Human.* New York, NY: St. Martin's Press.

Smith, M. 2010. Beyond the error theory. In R. Joyce and S. Kirchin, eds., *A World Without Values: Essays on John Mackie's Error Theory.* Dordrecht, Holland: Springer, 2010: 119–39.

Sober, E. 1981. The evolution of rationality. *Synthese* 46: 95–120.

——1984. *The Nature of Selection.* Cambridge, MA: MIT Press.

Sosa, E. 1993. Proper functionalism and virtue epistemology. *Noûs* 27: 51–65.

——1999. How to defeat opposition to Moore. *Philosophical Perspectives* 13: 141–53.

——2005. Tracking, competence, and knowledge. In P. K. Moser, ed., *The Oxford Handbook of Epistemology.* Oxford: Oxford University Press, 2005: 264–86.

Stich, S. 1990. *The Fragmentation of Reason.* Cambridge, MA: MIT Press.

Street, S. 2006. A Darwinian dilemma for realist theories of value. *Philosophical Studies* 127: 109–66.

——2008. Constructivism about reasons. *Oxford Studies in Metaethics* 3: 207–45.

——Objectivity and truth: you'd better rethink it. [Unpublished ms.]

Stroud, B. 1981. Evolution and the necessities of thought. Reprinted in *Meaning, Understanding, and Practice.* Oxford: Oxford University Press, 2000: 52–66.

Sturgeon, N. 1988. Moral explanations. In G. Sayre-McCord, ed., *Essays on Moral Realism.* Ithaca, NY: Cornell University Press, 1988: 229–55.

——2002. Ethical intuitionism and ethical naturalism. In P. Stratton-Lake, ed., *Ethical Intuitionism.* Oxford: Oxford University Press, 2002: 184–211.

——2009. Doubts about the supervenience of the ethical. *Oxford Studies in Metaethics* 4: 53–90.

Thompson, M. 2008. *Life and Action.* Cambridge, MA: Harvard University Press.

Turnbull, C. 1972. *The Mountain People.* New York, NY: Simon and Schuster.

Unger, P. 1968. An analysis of factual knowledge. *Journal of Philosophy* 65: 157–70.

van Fraassen, B. 1984. Belief and the will. *Journal of Philosophy* 81: 235–56.

Weatherson, B. 2007. The Bayesian and the dogmatist. *Proceedings of the Aristotelian Society* 107: 169–85.

Wedgwood, R. 2002. Internalism explained. *Philosophy and Phenomenological Research* 65: 349–69.

——2007. *The Nature of Normativity.* Oxford: Oxford University Press.

——2010. The moral evil demons. In R. Feldman and T. Warfield, eds., *Disagreement.* Oxford: Oxford University Press, 2010: 216–46.

——forthcoming. A priori bootstrapping. In A. Casullo and J. Thurow, eds., *The A Priori in Philosophy.* Oxford: Oxford University Press.

White, R. 2006. Problems for dogmatism. *Philosophical Studies* 131: 525–57.

Wiggins, D. 1987. A sensible subjectivism? In *Needs, Values, Truth.* Oxford: Blackwell, 1987: 185–214.

Williams, B. 1979. Internal and external reasons. Reprinted in *Moral Luck.* Cambridge: Cambridge University Press, 1981: 101–13.

——1985. *Ethics and the Limits of Philosophy.* Cambridge, MA: Harvard University Press.

——1993. *Shame and Necessity.* Berkeley, CA: University of California Press.

Williamson, T. 2000. *Knowledge and its Limits.* Oxford: Oxford University Press.

——2003. Understanding and inference. *Proceedings of the Aristotelian Society, Supplementary Volume* 77: 249–93.

——2007. *The Philosophy of Philosophy.* Oxford: Blackwell.

Wright, C. 1988. Moral values, projection and secondary qualities. *Proceedings of the Aristotelian Society, Supplementary Volume* 62: 1–26.

——2004. Warrant for nothing (and foundations for free). *Proceedings of the Aristotelian Society, Supplementary Volume* 78: 167–212.

Wright, L. 1973. Functions. *Philosophical Review* 82: 139–68.

——1976. *Teleological Explanation.* Berkeley, CA: University of California Press.

Yablo S. 1992. Mental causation. *Philosophical Review* 101: 245–80.

Yamada, M. 2011. Getting it right by accident. *Philosophy and Phenomenological Research* 83: 72–105.

Zimmerman, A. 2010. *Moral Epistemology.* London: Routledge.

INDEX

undermining; inference;
knowledge

Quine, W. V. 105 n. 39

rational egoism, *see* egoism, rational
Rawls, J. 26–7
realism, ethical 3, 6, 57, 68–83, 111–14,
    115–16 n. 57
    see also constitutive independence;
    Platonism
Reductionism 6, 10, 58, 99, 112–15,
    118–20, 125, 131, 132 n. 8, 144–6
    see also Platonism; reductive
    naturalism
Reductive Epistemology 49–65, 75–8,
    81–3, 87, 93–4, 113–14, 140, 148
reductive naturalism 8–11
    see also Reductionism
Reflection 33–9, 61
reflective equilibrium 2, 5, 15, 23–7, 82–3
    see also Empirical Model; intuitions,
    ethical; Pure Coherence View
relativism 2, 3–4, 6–7, 8, 13, 84, 123–9,
    134–8, 151–6
    see also convergence; disagreement;
    reliability, natural
reliability 1–2, 4, 5–7, 55–7, 63–6, 87–8,
    102–3
    natural 7, 142–4, 146–58
    see also coincidence; convergence;
    disagreement; knowledge
Revised Empirical Model 32–6, 39
Richard, M. 4 n. 3
Richerson, P., *see* Boyd R. and
    Richerson, P.
Rohrbaugh, G., *see* Neta, R. and
    Rohrbaugh, G.
Rosen, G., *see* Burgess, J. and Rosen, G.
Ross, W. D. 41 n. 33, 42 n. 36, 46 n., 111 n.
Russell, B. 9 n. 10

safety 89–93, 97–9
Sainsbury, M. 89 n. 5
Sawyer, S., *see* Majors, B. and Sawyer, S.
Sayre-McCord, G. 25–6, 27 n. 22, 36
Scanlon, T. M. 14 n. 8, 26 n., 111 n.
scepticism 1–8, 12, 15, 17–23, 27–41, 45, 47,
    50, 52–5, 99–100, 138, 142 n., 157–8
    see also coincidence; convergence;
    genetic undermining; knowledge
Schafer, K. 68 n., 71 n. 22, 74 n.

Schiffer, S. 61 n. 6
sentimentalism 143
Setiya, K. 27 n. 23, 115–16 n. 57, 135 n. 13
Shafer-Landau, R. 41 n. 33, 42 n. 34, 46
    n., 65 n. 13, 111 n.
Shaver, R. 14 n. 4
Sidgwick, H. 12, 14, 17, 41
Silins, N. 110 n. 47, 110 n. 49
Sinnott-Armstrong, W. 42–3, 87
slavery 1–2, 9, 138, 142, 152–3
Smith, D. L. 152
Smith, M. 118 n. 61
Sober, E. 106–8
Social Constructivism 126–7,
    134, 154–5
    see also constructivism
Social Externalism 125–9, 134, 154–5
    see also externalism
Sosa, E. 89 n. 5, 91 n. 7, 92 nn. 10–11,
    109 n. 45
Stich, S. 105 n. 39
Street, S. 6 n., 57 n. 1, 66, 69–71, 76–8,
    81–3, 112 n., 114 n. 54, 116–18
Stroud, B. 71 n. 21, 85–7
Sturgeon, N. 8 n. 7, 9 n. 9, 42, 49 n. 46,
    58–9
supervenience 4–5, 8–13, 31, 40, 49, 54–5,
    65, 114, 148
Swampman 109 n. 45

teleology 98, 105–12
testimony 25–6, 35–6, 39–40, 56, 73–4,
    140
Thompson, M. 108 n. 44, 130–2, 133 n.,
    135 n. 12, 136, 146
Turnbull, C. 150 n. 31

Unger, P. 89

van Fraassen, B. 33 n.
violence 150–2

Weatherson, B. 50 n. 48, 61 n. 8
Wedgwood, R. 14 n. 3, 35 n., 62 n.,
    93 n. 13, 109 n. 46, 114 n. 53,
    118–19, 122
White, R. 33 n., 45 n., 50 n. 48, 61 nn.
    6–7, 80 n. 29
Wiggins, D. 143 n. 22